Contents

KU-243-434

Acknowledgements

Without the help of the following this book could not have been written:

Johnnie Johnson
Howard Gillings
Keith Palmer
Dee Vickery
Eddie Rigby
Natalie Andrews
Audrey Gregory
Barrie Wade
Angel Scott
Bob Moy
Trevor Dickinson
John Taylor HMI
Chris Vallance
Julian Bowker
David Allen
Oonagh Cox
Steve Cooper
Dave Cath
Andrew Stibbs
Kate Fleming
Ken Wilby
Nick Roberts
Julie Warne

I would also like to express my appreciation to Henrietta Dombey for her help with the section on testing; to Richard Renée for his contribution to the DARTS workshop and to Johnnie Johnson, Peter Neale, Norman Owens and the Southern Area Language Co-ordinators' Support Group, West Sussex.

General editor's introduction

A great deal has happened since I wrote the Introduction to the first edition of this book in 1988. At the time the original text was published, we were just beginning to feel the effects of the publication in May 1988 of the Report of the Kingman Inquiry into English Language Teaching. Subsequently, of course, we have had the establishment of the National Curriculum in England and Wales with the Working Party that laid down the game plan for this in terms of English under the Chairmanship of Professor Brian Cox being told by the then Secretary of State to build upon the foundations laid by the Report of the Kingman Inquiry.

The Postscript to the first edition was entitled 'Interpreting Kingman' and was written by Richard Knott who was himself a member of the Committee of Inquiry. Not surprisingly the present volume brings this all up to date by its reference to the Cox Working Party's Report, *English for Ages 5–16* and it is interesting that so many of the conclusions reached after Kingman can remain more or less intact in the 1990s.

However, there is one very important general addition to the list of conclusions about language as it now reads. That is in the recognition that 'teachers and pupils need a shared language for talking about language, that is – a meta-language'. It seems surprising that in 1988 this should have been one of the most hotly contested findings of the Kingman Inquiry with many teachers of English fearing that what this really meant was a return by devious means to some kind of formal grammar teaching. That Cox did not recommend this and that his Report placed language teaching squarely within the more liberal traditions of good English teaching came as a great relief to the bulk of the English teaching profession. Since then, the concept of Knowledge about Language (KAL) has become firmly established as one of the key concepts underlying the work of English teachers in relation to the National Curriculum. It is significant how much work has been done since then in this area to which this series has made a distinctive contribution, especially in the publication of the work of Mittins (1990), Keen (1992), and Shepherd (1993).

However, Cox himself has shown that nothing to do with language can ever be seen as a neutral matter and the battles that raged in 1991 over the political interference with the publication of the material from the Language in the National Curriculum (LINC) project illustrated this very well. Since the bulk of this material has now been published we can see that the government overreacted to what have proved, in terms of in-service work, very useful materials indeed. The controversy that was engendered did more than anything else to make teachers (and increasingly parents and governors) aware of language as a live issue.

The fact that the present volume is going into a second edition indicates how much teachers still feel a need for guidance about the important area of language and this is even more true now than when the first edition was published. Indeed, it is no exaggeration to suspect that the original volume was one of the many forces in the late 1980s that was beginning to shift the focus of the English curriculum firmly in the direction of language study in the widest sense of the term. When, in 1988, we were awaiting the first publications for the guidelines for the English National Curriculum, I signalled the original book as being a major contribution in the debate that was just beginning and hoped that its outcome would demonstrate 'the scholarship, the concern for individual children, the humane sense of values, and (above all) the tentativeness of tone of the present authors'. On the whole the outcome of events since then have proved that this has been the case and we have been lucky. That is so far; at the time of writing we now await the promised revisions of English in the National Curriculum with something like the apprehension with which we awaited its original birth in 1988.

However, also in introducing the first edition, I suggested that readers were likely to be encouraged by 'the robust attitude to language teaching adopted by the present authors'. I see no reason to change that view now.

'Knowledge about Language' was mentioned earlier and it is significant of how the times have changed that no mention of that phrase was made in my introduction to the first edition. Instead I reminded readers of the recommendation to all schools in the Bullock Report, *A Language for Life* (1975), of the adoption of a 'language policy across the curriculum'. Kingman reinforced this argument with a specific recommendation that all primary schools should have a member of staff designated as a language consultant, with the responsibility for advising on and co-ordinating language work. Now with the advent of the National Curriculum this becomes even more important and the work of such a co-ordinator needs to extend beyond teacher, pupil and classroom to the ever-increasingly important area of communication with governors and parents.

The other thing that has become of increasing importance in England and Wales as a result of the introduction of the National Curriculum has been the area of continuity in student learning between primary and secondary school. It is hoped, therefore, that the present volume, like its predecessor, will be found useful to those having the responsibility for handling the transition between the various stages of education.

The author has continued to show his scholarship in bringing the book up to date and there are many new references for which room has had to be found. In terms of assessment at the time of writing we do not yet know what the final form will be of this at Key Stages 1 and 2 (ages 7 and 11) with which the book is mainly concerned. What does seem certain is that students taught in schools where the principles about language teaching espoused in this book are put into practice will be well prepared for whatever awaits them. They will also, in the words of the title of the Bullock Report, have been well prepared in their primary schooling with 'A Language for Life'.

Anthony Adams

The author has continued to show his scholarship in bringing the book up to date and there are many new references for which room has had to be found. In terms of assessment at the time of writing we do not yet know what the final form will be of this at Key Stages 1 and 2 (ages 7 and 11) with which the book is mainly concerned. What does seem certain is that students taught in schools where the principles about language teaching espoused in this book are put into practice will be well prepared for whatever awaits them. They will also, in the words of the title of the Bullock Report, have been well prepared in their primary schooling with 'A Language for Life'.

Anthony Adams

1 What should the post-holder do?

Joyce Hargreaves has been teaching for fifteen years at the Hangleton Road First and Middle School. Following her training, she took up her post at Hangleton Road and, apart from a break of eight years, when she was involved in the bringing up of a young family, she has worked at the school ever since. In her own words, she has seen it all! 'One bandwagon follows another, like night follows day', she can be heard to sigh when the details of another in-service course on the teaching of reading are pinned to the staffroom notice-board. Or sometimes she'll say to her friend of long-standing, Betty Wilkins, 'If we stay as we are, things will move full circle, you mark my words. Who's going to check we're doing this National Curriculum anyway?' By this time the unfortunate and recently discovered details of Kevin Pettigrew's hearing problems have been pinned on top of the sheet listing in-service courses.

Joyce Hargreaves works very hard. She marks thoroughly in red pen, has a well-ordered formal classroom, plans her work carefully and knows the children. Indeed, she taught some of their parents, as did Betty Wilkins.

Joyce and Betty felt comfortable with Mr Chasemore, who retired from the headship of Hangleton Road some eighteen months ago. They are not so sure about Ms Jackson: 'Why is she "Ms" and why does she want to turn a good school, which is popular with the parents, upside down? All of this theory is so much nonsense. Most of these trendy ideas don't actually work in the classroom.'

Liz Jackson's brief from the Local Authority was 'to get Hangleton Road moving!' Owing to retirements, she has been lucky enough to appoint a good probationer and a lively, experienced teacher to assume responsibility for mathematics. She feels that the language work in the school fails to develop the children's abilities; it is, she claims, based too firmly on course books and 'a rather dull reading scheme'. The head realizes that Joyce and Betty have many sterling qualities and doesn't want to 'throw the baby out with the bathwater', but she is worried about the nature of some of the work going on in their classrooms. She is also aware that they form an influential axis in the staffroom – and that they are not likely to leave!

One member of her staff has recently completed a part-time diploma course in language development and reading and can be given the remaining point to take on the post of language consultant.

Although written with a certain sense of irony, the situation which we have outlined above may not be totally unfamiliar! There is a new, forward-looking, thrusting headteacher bent on changing curriculum content and classroom practice. There are one or two confident teachers who are fully prepared to look critically at their own work and, if necessary, change classroom practice in line with the demands of the National Curriculum. There are one or two doubters who prefer to avoid the challenge of change. And then – there are Joyce and Betty!

What does the post-holder for language development do?
Where does she or he start? What are the priorities?

There is little doubt that the role of the language post-holder is extremely onerous. She or he is seen as an agent of change who often carries very little extra status within the school. Furthermore, language development goes further than National Curriculum English. It is not a clearly defined curriculum area, but rather, it underpins all of the learning which takes place in the school. Indeed, it is interesting to note that some headteachers, recognizing the two points above, have taken on this demanding role themselves.

Since language development and effective learning are inextricably linked, then it follows that the language post-holder will soon be drawn into discussions concerning the way the classrooms of colleagues are managed.

'Language' is not something which can be tacked on to existing classroom activities; 'Language' is not the 'English' of secondary schools with the literature shorn off; 'Language' is not merely the aggregation of reading scheme, spelling policy, comprehension exercises, handwriting and marking strategies stapled together in the form of a talisman to ward off marauding inspectors. The child's language is the medium through which she or he learns.

Many in-service courses are aimed at telling post-holders what they need to know about language. Few are concerned with how post-holders can introduce ideas to their colleagues in such a way that they will use them and continue to use them. The activities in this book are designed to fit a school-based model of curriculum development and in-service training; we believe that is the most effective way of working.

Choosing priorities

Below are listed a number of activities which a newly appointed post-holder might consider. Give yourself fifteen minutes to place these in order of priority:

- a new reading scheme
- new language course book(s)
- additional fiction
- a thematic approach
- handwriting skills
- group work
- marking strategies
- develop reading comprehension
- display of children's writing
- buy SRA
- get rid of SRA
- write a language document
- home–school liaison
- develop listening skills
- a four-session in-service course run by you over a term
- working with the most resistant teacher(s)
- working with the most encouraging teacher(s)
- getting professional writers into school
- organize a book/story/poetry week
- teaching poetry
- getting rid of language course books
- assessment profiles
- new objective tests
- go on a course
- look for another job
- surveying what goes on
- distribute *English from 5 to 16*
- try to find a copy of the Bullock Report
- prepare teaching materials
- mug up on Piaget, Vygotsky, Graves, Barnes, Smith and so on
- go to the pub/wine bar
- use microcomputers
- try to tighten up punctuation work/spelling/basic skills
- draw a grid of National Curriculum Attainment Targets
- map what you're already doing from the Programmes of Study
- buy Knowledge about Language textbooks.

There is, of course, no 'correct' answer, though teachers usually put 'Finding out' as their first choice: you need to know what is happening in classrooms throughout the school.

Finding out

List as many strategies as you can think of which will enable you to gauge what is going on in colleagues' classrooms:

1 Ask them . . .
2
3
4

How many of these could you use with all the staff?

One problem which may emerge is that judgements can be formed based on what people say is happening in their classrooms. However, the learning which is actually taking place may not match the teacher's expectations or hopes. The real curriculum is what the children take away from the learning experience. This may be less (or more) than is realized; it will certainly be different.

The child's learning

What strategies exist for finding out what the children have learned and what they think they have learned?

Let us return for a moment to Betty and Joyce who are likely to be highly suspicious about most, if not all, of the strategies you have suggested. Do their opinions contain anything which could be of use to the post-holder? One thing is certain: they will be hostile to theory which appears to have no foundation in classroom realities, and wary of new opportunities which they feel have only temporary validity. In short, they would not take on trust the suggestions made by the post-holder. Classroom activity must have a clearly thought-out theoretical foundation; teachers ought to know why they want their classes to work in a particular way, and it is for the post-holder to help translate appropriate theory into workable classroom practice. Joyce and Betty need to see clearly articulated theory working successfully in the classroom. It follows that the post-holder's classroom should be available as a model of good practice; ideally, too, a significant part of the post-holder's role should be concerned with the initiation and collation of materials for use in classrooms throughout the school. They should embody a coherent and supportive language policy.

As 9-year-old Daniel Harvey observed:

> We sit on the carpet and Mr Gibson comes in, and he sits down in his chair and says 'Right, we're going to do language' and I groan to myself because I don't like language. It's boring. He tells us to do Section 11, Book 3, and we go and sit down with our books which we fight over for about fifteen minutes. Mr Gibson always says, 'Fifteen minutes ago I was talking about language, why are there forty-three people wandering about?'[1]

Language isn't something you 'do'; it isn't appropriate to adopt the 'cricket net' approach to language learning. We hope, in this book, to make the search for a coherent and supportive language policy one in which the post-holder will play a major role, but also one in which all staff share – and from which the children benefit.

2 Speaking and listening

It is no accident that speaking and listening is Attainment Target 1 in National Curriculum English.

An LEA Inspector

Through the programme of study, pupils should encounter a range of situations, audiences and activities which are designed to develop their competence, precision and confidence in speaking and listening, irrespective of their initial competence or home language.

Programme of Study 2 – General Introduction

Quiet there. This is a language lesson so there should be no talking *at all*.

From Gene Kemp, *Charlie Lewis Plays for Time*[1]

The supply teacher at Gene Kemp's Cricklepit Combined School knows what he likes: a class rigidly divided into ability groups; course books with joyless titles like 'New and Improved English for Primary Schools'; and children who can maintain an orderly silence. This doesn't fool Charlie Lewis, of course; the lesson is one of 'quiet miserable boredom'! Not only are such classrooms boring, they also deny children the opportunity to use language in a way that develops their ability to shape the totality of their experience. Schools where the playground bears witness to the vigour of children's talk, but the classrooms are hushed, have cut away something very important. It is no coincidence that we have placed this section on talk so early in the book; there is little dispute now that its position is central: 'anyone who succeeded in outlawing talk in the classroom would have outlawed life',[2] was the way James Britton put it years before the Bullock Report (DES, 1975). The poet, Tony Harrison, has eloquently pointed to the consequence of inarticulateness:

The dumb go down in history and disappear
and not one gentleman's been brought to book:
Mes den hep tavas a-gollas y dyr
(Cornish) –
'the tongueless man gets his land took.'[3]

Key statement	Question
We learn by making mistakes; meaning comes before precision.	How is the classroom organized to enable that to happen?
The child's language must be accepted and acted upon.	How can the *individual* child be valued?
Children develop as language learners by trying to *do* something.	How can such activities be made as *real* as possible?
Adults provide the models.	What constitutes a 'good' model?
We should create a variety of purposes and audiences.	How?
The 'quality' of the language they encounter matters.	What constitutes 'quality'?

Figure 2.1   Key statements and related questions about 'good language development'

Children are entitled to a curriculum which consciously sets out to develop children's language, making them capable, giving them power. Much of what we have to say about talk, applies no less to language itself. Take, for example, the key statements about 'good language development'[4] and the related questions in Figure 2.1.

Clearly 'Talk' and 'Language' are interchangeable here – inevitably, since the various language areas are so enmeshed. As the National Curriculum reminds us: 'The profile components are inter-related. Because of the inter-relationship between language modes, in good classroom practice the programmes of study will necessarily and rightly be integrated' (POS into Practice B1). Consequently it would be naive to plan for separate 'spoken English', therefore, since children should move freely through the language domains, talking, reading, listening and writing as the situation demands. Our separate emphasis here is to reinforce the central position of the spoken word.

English from 5 to 16[5] and its more humane and logical offspring *English from 5 to 16: The Responses*[6] were in no doubt about the importance of talk. The latter document commented that many readers of the former 'perceived . . . what they regarded as a strengthened emphasis upon the importance of the spoken word'. Regrettably, though, the original booklet laid undue emphasis on objectives, identified for the three apparently significant ages of 7, 11 and 16. It is an interesting and salutary exercise for a school staff to take the following objectives, drawn from *English from 5 to 16* and attempt to estimate the age at which they think 'most pupils' can achieve what is defined (the objectives have been 'mixed up' here and the Inspectorate's version is included in the notes[7]).

- Converse confidently and pleasantly in social situations.
- Describe clearly experience they have undergone.

- Make clear statements of fact.
- Frame pertinent questions.
- Explain what they are doing when involved in a task.
- Speak in role in dramatic play.
- Make and take telephone calls, giving and receiving information accurately.
- Argue a case.
- Express ideas and feelings accurately.
- Describe what they have observed.
- Use the resources of the voice (modulation, tone, etc.) expressively.
- Use gesture and movement in association with the voice when effective communication demands it.
- Give short talks on matters of which they have knowledge.

The fact that, in all probability, the staff will be unable to reach a consensus does not reflect badly upon them! Rather it makes a mockery of pedantic attempts to pigeon-hole the intangible. I know 6 year olds well able to 'make and take telephone calls' and at least one 41 year old who finds it a struggle, on occasions, to 'argue a case'! It all depends, of course, on the case to be argued and with whom; or who is telephoning whom and for what purpose. Undeniably, too, you cannot separate talking from listening: real conversations do not occur in that kind of limbo. After all speaking and listening comprise one profile component not two!

The spoken language club[8]

Frank Smith's description of the way infants learn to talk is striking and important: 'Infants join a spoken-language club with a single unqualified reciprocal act of affiliation. There are no dues to be paid, no entry standards to be met, and there is no demand for references.' Most of them learn easily and naturally. The learning is, again in Smith's words:[9]

- meaningful
- useful
- continual and effortless
- incidental
- collaborative
- vicarious
- free of risk.

We all learn most effectively in such circumstances. The talk which teachers foster in classrooms should reflect those characteristics; failure to plan for them must lead to classroom language which is listless, artificial and repetitive.

What sort of talk?

'I feel that I don't allow children to talk enough in both formal and informal ways . . . I always feel constrained to produce something in writing.' This remark is not

THE CHILD SHOULD HAVE THE OPPORTUNITY TO:	With one other member of staff, identify an occasion in the past week when you have enabled the children to talk in that way . . .

With one other member of staff, identify an occasion in the past week when you have enabled the children to talk in that way . . .

- ask relevant questions
- tell and listen to stories
- persuade others
- share ideas
- encourage others
- speculate
- negotiate (and make concessions!)
- give (and act on) instructions
- make decisions and reach judgements
- summarize ideas
- think aloud
- reflect on their effectiveness in speaking and listening
- fine tune talk to fit audience and purpose.

Figure 2.2   Kinds of talk

untypical; it points to the need for greater certainty about what kinds of talk and the contexts in the classroom in which talk should take place (see Figure 2.2), and the requirements of the programmes of study for speaking and listening in the non-statutory guidance.

Talk needs to be natural; the context needs to seem real; the purpose must be clear. The children need to feel free to take risks and confident that any contribution they make is valued. In the following extract, the class of third-year juniors had been taken by their teacher deep into a simulation in which a mysterious house is being sold. By this point, both Simon and the children asking the questions 'believe' in what they are doing:[10]

Darren: What was it like at night when you were in bed?
Simon: Well, it was a bit creepy. [*Pause*]
Lucy: Did you hear any noises in the loft?
Simon: No, only really rats. [*Pause*]

John: Do the radiators make noises?
Simon: Not all the time.
Gill: Do the stairs really creak?

Simon: No.
Wayne: Had you actually heard any screaming or anything?
Simon: Only next-door neighbours.
Wayne: Can you hear the thermostat at night when the water's warming up?
Simon: No . . .
Lucy: Do the floorboards squeak at night?
Wanda: Was there sort of noise from under the floorboards? As if someone was
           under them?
Simon: No . . .
Carla: Did you hear things that go bump in the night?

The questioning is intense and pertinent and the absorption of the children in the activity is similarly impressive; it is significant how much listening is going on. Although the talk is exploratory and tentative, there are moments when silence falls and you can sense the shared thinking. Arguably, these children could not have devised such a barrage of questions without the benefit of the role-play structure devised by the teacher. Her work stimulated the committed response from the children and she has the confidence and wit to keep a low profile through much of the subsequent discussion.

Case study: contexts for talk

For the classroom teacher, the important points to carry over into daily practice are that the spoken word should feature as a natural and substantial part of learning, that both talking and listening should occur and that they should usually be integrated; that they should frequently occur in conjunction with the other language modes (reading and writing) and that, wherever possible, they should be employed for 'real or realistic purposes' in the curriculum.[11]

How does the teacher's experience and perceptions outlined below match the preceding paragraph?

I teach at a multi-racial school just outside London and my current class consists of thirty-two 7 and 8 year olds. I am very keen that the children should be encouraged to think aloud, to take chances, to trust me and each other. I use groupwork a lot, but I shift the groups regularly, sometimes exploiting friendship patterns and, at other times, expecting them to work with others in the class. Hopefully, I am alert to those boys who tend to dominate groups! Occasionally, I use tape recorders in an attempt to raise the status of their talk. More often, it is clear from the activity that talking is crucial for its own sake – for example, we could be discussing models that are in construction, or paintings; giving instructions to another group; devising a programme of stories and poems for an audience of parents, or younger children; solving a Maths problem. In all such cases, I would hope that the children's talk is about decisions they must make for their work to proceed. I'm not interested in decontextualized 'class discussion' where it's all too easy for kids to retreat into themselves and let the lesson drift over them.

We also talk about talk! I want them to think about language and to reflect on why we do what we do. I think that's really important. Above all, in my planning of our work I battle to set up situations where the children talk because they must: real contexts and real audiences.

Contexts for talk: a checklist[12]

What follows in Figure 2.3 is a starting point only; there are many other possibilities which staff can – and should – discuss. In taking this further, it would be useful to refer to the checklist in Figure 2.2. and, of course, the National Curriculum programmes of study.

Kinds of talk[13]	Suggested context
• Formulation of questions	See pages 10–11. When the children genuinely wish to know the answer.
• Telling a story	Prior to a small group writing and illustrating it for another (younger?) audience.
• Persuasion	When the persuader really cares about the effects of his or her persuasion, for example about a course of action that is dependent upon the outcome of the discussion.
• Giving directions	To someone who really needs the information.
• Adopts a role	Within a dramatic simulation, or as an 'expert' to the teacher-in-role as 'skilful ignoramus'.[14]
• Explains a process	Perhaps during the making of something.

Figure 2.3   Suggested contexts for different kinds of talk

It is deceptively easy to assume that the teacher's contribution to classroom talk can be relatively laid-back: Martin Coles in an article entitled 'Hearing a Pin Drop? An Examination of Small Group Discussion with Seven Year Olds'[15] writes an interesting account of such classroom activity:

> I found the complexity of interactions between the children startling. And yet the surprising thing was that I had done very little to foster such interaction. I had simply provided an opportunity and a specific context for discussion.

The children had been reading *The Shrinking of Treehorn* by Florence Parry Heide[16] and the teacher had 'simply' put the children in groups of four and instructed them to 'ask each other questions about the book'. What can be forgotten, however, is the teacher's role in choosing the right context at the right time: such a skill is an important one since it determines the level of commitment of the children; it also presupposes a realistic and objective knowledge of the individual members of the class. The teacher's judgement of pupils and context is crucial. As Coles writes:

> The Treehorn tapes convinced me that young children are capable of the whole range of human thinking if the context is right. They can produce imaginative ideas, attempt to solve problems, explore implications, explain, predict, interpret, express feelings, reason logically, justify an opinion, and unselfconsciously find it all fun, if only they are given proper opportunities.

Planning the context

'Am I being fair to the children?'!

- Are the questions that I've asked 'open-ended' or closed?
- Do the questions I ask 'push on' the thinking of the children?
- Is the problem posed a genuine one with a genuine solution?
- Do I use what the pupils offer?
- Am I tolerant of children's anecdotes, or do I always keep control of what is 'relevant'?
- Are children encouraged to share ideas, to pool information?
- Are children given clear 'agendas' and time targets to sharpen the focus of their talk?
- Is time given to allow children to establish and confirm their understanding through talk?
- Can both sexes contribute to discussion on an equal footing?
- Do I recognize that listening is difficult and plan accordingly?
- Do I provide a model as a listener? Do I listen?

Listening skills

It is as misguided to teach listening skills in isolation as it is to give no thought to the contexts in which pupils' talk occurs. Talking and listening are bound together too closely for us to practise them independently: when talking happens you need to know that someone is listening; to listen properly you need to care about what is being said. Children who 'never listen' may merely reflect the fact that their experience hitherto has led them to the conclusion that there's nothing worth hearing! It is not an easy skill to acquire however; how often in adult conversation are we aware that words are tumbling out into a void? We need to struggle to ensure that children learn to listen to each other; Harold Gardiner commented:

> People listen best when they have a real purpose for listening (when they have a stake in the activity); in real discussion in which the teacher's contribution (if any) . . . is not over-authoritarian; pre-discussion and post-discussion of any activity in language; children talking as experts to genuine listeners; children listening to tapes and responding to the talk features contained in them . . . these are just some kinds of activity which emphasise but don't isolate listening.[17]

Figure 2.4 Discussion techniques: some starting points

TECHNIQUES	STARTING POINTS					
	BOOKS	EXPERIENCE	THE VISUAL	HARDWARE	DRAMA	USING THE GROUP
	'Language develops where roots and reading cross'	PREPARED TALKS About hobbies, personal news, etc.	USE OF PHOTOGRAPHS As a stimulus, e.g. mount a photo on a large piece of white card and group writes questions around the edges.	TAPE Of plays/ drama scripts Interviews Recording information Programme making Anthologies	ROLE PLAY IMPROVISATION SIMULATION	BRAINSTORMING Making a list without discussion. One group member takes notes; everyone contributes
	DARTS Close Prediction Sequencing etc.	STARTING FROM THE CHILDREN Valuing and using: the anecdote stories jokes	USE OF PICTURES INTERPRETATIONS Give each group some visual material; they must agree on a written statement or caption.	USE OF TV, VIDEO FILM COMPUTERS For collaborative talk	See Chapter 6, on Drama	QUESTIONING of each other of visitors of you BOARD GAMES (devising) ASSEMBLIES (planning)
	See Chapter 4, on reading			See pages 79–81		RANKING Agreeing an order for a list of items or ideas. Can be presented as a diamond formation
	LITERATURE A rich source for talk					SEQUENCING PREDICTION Not just of text, but of events, behaviour (science, history)
	See pages 15–17					ATTACKING A PROBLEM In maths, science – MOVING FROM GROUP TO PLENARY AND BACK

Again, we return to the crucial importance of the teacher's intervention, planning and technique.

Discussion techniques

What experience has the staff got of the techniques referred to in Figure 2.4?

Talk and literature

Nothing will come of nothing. Our developing articulateness comes in large measure from the words that resound in and around us; those, in turn, come most forcefully from literature. We deal elsewhere with 'reading', but it is valuable to remind ourselves of how the written word, the shared emotion, the power of story, can stimulate and feed both instant vocal response and, more broadly, the way we use language throughout our lives. Literature gives access to the power of language. Ezra Pound argued that literature was a way of keeping words living and accurate; for Kafka, 'a book or a poem must be an ice-axe to break the sea frozen inside us'. In classrooms, a book or a poem can unlock talk that is genuinely exploratory and drama can provide the context for this imaginative examination of texts to take place.

EXAMPLE 1

About Friends

The good thing about friends
Is not having to finish sentences.

I sat a whole summer afternoon with my friend once
on a river bank, bashing heels on the baked mud
and watching the small chunks slide into the water
and listening to them – plop plop plop.
He said 'I like the twigs when they . . . you know . . .
like that.' I said 'There's that branch . . .'
We both said 'Mmmmm'. The river flowed and flowed
and there were lots of butterflies, that afternoon.

I first thought there was a sad thing about friends
when we met twenty years later.
We both talked hundreds of sentences
taking care to finish all we said,
and explain it all very carefully,
as if we'd been discovered in places
we should not be, and were somehow ashamed.

I understood then what the river meant by flowing.

Brian Jones

Four pupils (in a self-selected friendship group) were asked to read the poem and then talk about what they found interesting or difficult to understand.[18] The teacher was not with them.

Surprisingly, perhaps, they cover a lot of ground in a relatively short discussion (far more than in a 'conventional' setting). The poem stimulates response: the children recognize the feeling at the heart of it:

> *Mark:*   I know a bit I don't understand.
> *David:*   What?
> *Mark:*   Last line on the second paragraph . . . third paragraph – 'we should not be, and were somehow ashamed . . .'
> *David:*   No . . . 'cos that feels like they was little doing this by the river banks.
> *Darren:* Yes – now they've got to do it all again . . . things have changed.
> *David:*   And they got caught sort of thing.
> *Mark:*   Ashamed of not knowing . . .
> *Darren:* Yeah . . . not knowing what they're going to say.
> *Paul:*   They feel ashamed of finishing their sentences because they're not like they were twenty years ago.
> *David:*   Yeah 'cos they think about the laugh and the joke . . .
> *Mark:*   Because they didn't understand each other . . .

In a poem about friendship and time gone, it is fascinating to hear four friends discussing lines like 'The good things about friends/Is not having to finish sentences' – and themselves finding no need to complete sentences.

EXAMPLE 2

> My ultimate aim with any of the children I teach is to help them become independent silent readers as quickly as possible. However, at the time when I actually sit down comfortably with a child to hear him or her read, my immediate intention is that we should have as relaxed and enjoyable time as we can: talking, reading, sharing, learning.[19]

Anne Baker's detailed, annotated transcript of such a conversation with 9-year-old Dawn in NATE's *Children Reading to Their Teachers* is a valuable model; one extract from the account (Figure 2.5) emphasizes many of my earlier points. The teacher is genuinely interested in the conversation; she prompts skilfully; values the child's thoughts and feelings; provides a good model as a listener. In addition, she is sending out some very strong signals about reading: not only is it something you can share and discuss, but it is pleasurable, important; furthermore, it helps all of us to rethink and clarify our view of the world and our role within it. From her reading of *Charlotte's Web*,[20] Dawn is encouraged to struggle with the unsettling notion of Charlotte's death; the language of the book and the shared conversation are all part of Dawn's growing 'way with words'.

Conversation	Teacher's comments
Teacher (T): Charlotte's Web Are you still thinking about it? *Dawn (D):* Yes. *T:* Go on. *D:* Thinking about when she died. *T:* Tell me about it. *D:* Well Wilbur was calling her and I think she fell off the wooden ledge bit and Wilbur started crying. I started crying then. *T:* Just then. *D:* Yes. Have you a favourite bit in *Charlotte's Web?* *T:* Who me? Mm. I think the bit I like the best is when Charlotte meets Wilbur for the first time and he hasn't seen her and . . . *D:* 'Wait until morning. You'll see me.' *T:* That's right 'Wait until morning and you'll see me.' And he wakes and he's very impatient when he wakes and then she says, 'Salutations'. And he doesn't know what it means 'Salut what?' he says. And then he does really meet her. I think that's my favourite bit. *D:* Mm. And she dies and when all her children hatch he says 'Salutations' to them. *T:* Yes he does, doesn't he. Do they understand him? *D:* No. *T:* They don't. *D:* Because these two children don't understand him. I like another bit when he called one of the spiders Nelly. *T:* Yes, that made me laugh too.	Dawn considers a book she's had difficulty coming to terms with. (This doesn't happen every time.) An open prompt to let Dawn specify her own area of concern. Now Dawn takes the initiative to make the conversation a genuinely shared experience.

Figure 2.5   Extract of annotated conversation with pupil

Talk and mathematics

The Cockcroft Report was insistent in its demand for opportunities for all pupils to talk through mathematical problems, both among themselves and with the teacher. In discussing Cockroft, one group of primary teachers made the conclusions tabulated in Figure 2.6.[21]

It would be an interesting exercise for a member of staff to look at the learning opportunities provided for pupils in mathematical work and, more specifically, to identify specific instances of some of the items in Figure 2.6. An obvious way into such a discussion would be the use of tape-recorders.

WHAT DOES DISCUSSION DO FOR:

The pupil?

- It allows the pupil to *personalize information*.
- It *consolidates ideas*.
- It helps a child to *clarify thoughts*.
- It helps a child *retain information*.
- It improves use of mathematical *vocabulary*.
- It helps a child to *solve problems*.
- It helps a child to *follow lines of enquiry*.
- It helps a child to relate abstract ideas to *concrete experience*.
- It encourages *confidence*.
- It encourages *self-help*.
- It makes maths more *enjoyable*.
- It encourages a *positive attitude*.

The teacher?

- It helps the teacher gain *awareness* of the child's strengths and weaknesses.
- It helps in *assessing* the level of real understanding.
- It allows the teacher to introduce *precise mathematical terms* in correct contexts.
- It helps in *planning* future work.
- It improves pupil–teacher *relationships*.
- It's easier to transmit *interest and enthusiasm*.
- It allows the teacher to '*make contact*' with the more timid, quieter child.

HOW CAN WE ACHIEVE THIS?

- By providing plenty of opportunities for discussion: Pupil–pupil, pupil–teacher.
- By setting up investigation and problem-solving situations.
- By creating a positive atmosphere.
- By being aware of the need to play, on occasions, a neutral, quieter role.

Figure 2.6   How discussion helps both pupil and teacher

Although the focus for Figure 2.6 is Mathematical, there is obviously much that is common to other areas of the curriculum within it. Figure 2.7 is intended to serve as an incentive to you to focus on that area of the curriculum which currently keeps you awake at night!

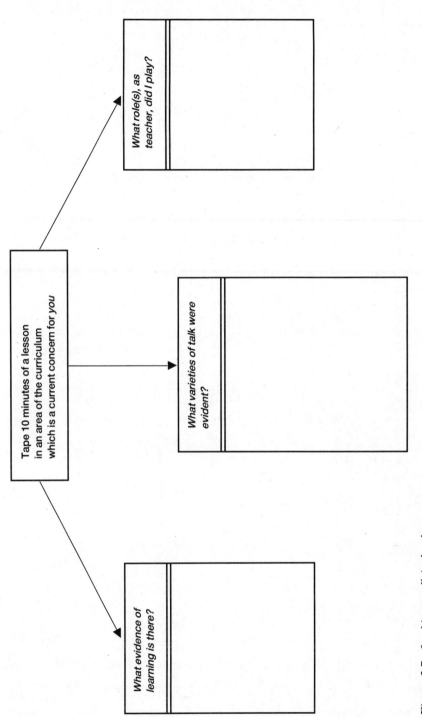

Figure 2.7 Looking at talk in the classroom

What do we do about . . . ?	Notes	Our next move should be . . .
1 ASSESSMENT	'Assessment ought to be task-embedded' – in other words, don't assess in isolation, or for its own sake.	(i) Is it possible to involve the pupils in assessing themselves? (ii) The purpose of the assessment should be clear.
2 GROUPWORK	'Groupwork should be the bedrock of talk in the classroom.'	(i) Develop the art of being sensitive to the needs and feelings of a group. (ii) Be aware of your position in the room and how it can affect the group's talk. (iii) Think hard about group composition.
3 RAISING THE STATUS OF TALK	'Talk should not be writing's rather disreputable cousin.'	(i) Talking doesn't have to end in writing. (ii) The children should know why their talk matters.
4 INTEGRATING TALK	'Oral work should not be something separate.'	Remember the importance of CONTEXT, AUDIENCE and PURPOSE.
5 FINDING THE RIGHT CONDITIONS TO RELEASE PUPIL TALK	'Putting a press on children's language.' 'Making a triangle of myself, the children and the activities outside both of us, but in which we are both involved for different reasons.'[22]	(i) Encourage use of the cassette (including the pause button!) (ii) Use adults other than teachers. (iii) Encourage tentativeness – spoken drafting. (iv) Find genuine audiences and purposes.
6 ACCENT AND DIALECT	'The language children bring with them from their home backgrounds should not be criticised, belittled or proscribed.'[23] 'Linguistically no accents are superior to any other.'[24]	(i) How important is 'standard English'? (ii) If it is important, when and how should it be taught?

Reference also needs to be made to other issues raised in earlier parts of this chapter.

Planning a policy for talk

> Although in about two-thirds of schools talking and listening were regarded as
> important aspects of the work, good practice more often depended on the initiatives
> of individual teachers than on the existence of agreed school policies.
>
> HMI survey[25]

School language policies vary enormously and may draw their inspiration from
sources 'as far apart as Bullock, *English from 5 to 16* and now the National
Curriculum programmes of study'. That part of the policy which deals with talk,
is all too often, sketchy and brief, while advice on writing is frequently daunting,
both in its length and complexity. Figure 2.8 is an attempt at mapping the
principal features which any policy needs to include. We have tried to design it in
such a way that it demands response from members of the school staff since it is
clear that a policy must stem from the combined experience and philosophy of the
staff. In that way there might be some match between what the staff says it does
and what actually happens day by day in the hurly-burly of individual classrooms.

Addressing these issues, should help to develop the school's existing policy for
talk.

Schools of eloquence

> I think the mark of somebody's real fluency in a language is their ability to switch
> from one set of circumstances to the next and make their language meet the
> demands of that context placed upon it.
>
> David Crystal[26]

Talk isn't just a classroom strategy; it isn't just about 'learning' in the narrow
sense. If the sound of silence in classrooms is the sound of consent 'There should
be no talking *at all*!', then talk is the means by which children – and adults –
become, in the best sense, powerful. The poet, Tony Harrison, in the opening
page of 'The School of Eloquence'[27] quotes E. P. Thompson:

> In 1799 special legislation was introduced 'utterly suppressing and prohibiting' by
> name the London Corresponding Society and the United Englishmen. Even the
> indefatigable conspirator, John Binns, felt that further national organisation was
> hopeless ... When arrested he was found in possession of a ticket which was
> perhaps one of the best 'covers' for the old LCS: Admit for the Season to the School
> of Eloquence.[28]

I believe that children and teachers should create around themselves 'Schools of
Eloquence' where the spoken word predominates.

Talk cannot be taught systematically, progressively, explicitly – though it helps
if children are aware of its purpose and nature, as shown below. It is not
appropriate to regard a sequence of work as 'oral work'; instead, it should be an
integral and inescapable part of classroom activity. Competence in talking stems
from teachers knowing how such competence blossoms; that is:[29]

● From adults and others attending to what is being said and responding
  accordingly.

- From thinking and working together.
- From a developing awareness that talk serves needs.
- From contact with mature speakers – adult time.
- From words to play with – patterns, play, routines.
- From challenge and involvement.
- From new and different contexts.
- From exploratory talk.

Sharing ideas

It is also important to plan ways for the pupils to share their ideas they have discussed in small groups with other members of the class. The most obvious strategy is the use of the spokesperson who summarizes what has been achieved. However, unless this is carefully handled it can become rather longwinded and, as one teacher ruefully put it, result in 'death by a thousand feedbacks'.

Two ways of overcoming this problem are through the use of Jigsaw groupings and envoying.

Jigsaw offers a flexible structure for group work.[30] There are 'home' and 'expert' groups.

With *home groups*, the teacher divides the whole class into small groups (commonly of four). These are set up by the teacher in order that each group reflects all the balances of the whole class – gender, race, ability, attitude. Each group is given a common task. Handouts are usually employed in order to set the task, but reading material is kept to a manageable length and complexity. If the home groups are of four, then there are four questions within the main task – one for each member of the group. The pupils themselves choose which questions they wish to concentrate on rather than being given them by the teacher.

With *expert groups*, all the pupils working on a particular question then regroup and work together on what is now a common problem, so that by the time this stage of the session is completed, each has become an expert on this matter with access to the combined ideas of the other experts within this new group. Original groups reform, that is they *return home*, each pupil having now become an 'expert' with something to say. The pupils also know that there will be a follow-up task requiring understanding of all four questions, not just their own speciality – the pieces of the jigsaw have to fit.

With envoying, each home group nominates an envoy who will join an adjacent group. Each envoy needs to be briefed clearly so that she or he can relay the home group's findings to the new group. The envoys then return to their home groups, feed in any new ideas or perspectives and compare these with the ideas brought to the home group by other envoys.

Detailed planning is, of course, vital if these approaches are to be effective. It is particularly important that the Jigsaw questions are carefully phrased so that they encourage discussion – yes or no answers aren't much use! As one teacher who has used Jigsaw extensively puts it:

We cannot sufficiently stress how imperative detailed planning is to the success of Jigsaw. Nor, after initial planning has been completed, can the teacher assume that their task has been accomplished. The nature of their role changes as the Jigsaw develops. As the children work within their Home and Expert groups the teacher will have opportunities to observe them at work and anticipate areas of difficulty. The teacher's response should be one of support without leading. Through open-ended questioning the children can be guided to a point where they can formulate their own decisions. To achieve this the teacher must be committed to the group work approach, realize its value as a teaching/learning style and have the confidence to experiment and learn from mistakes.

Summary

1 Oral work is an essential element in classroom activity. All pupils are entitled to work in classrooms where talking and listening are part of the natural order of things. Children – and adults too – learn effectively through talk. Consequently, the teacher has the considerable responsibility of devising situations and purposes which motivate pupils and which generate real communication. There should be a preparedness on the teacher's part to negotiate with pupils over the direction in which their learning is going and the kinds of talk that are most enabling.
2 Children's ability to talk develops through the range and complexity of the experiences in life and in school which they undergo. Silence in a classroom might indicate diligent scholarship; it is more likely to suggest an atmosphere in which children are not encouraged to talk about their writing or their reading; where language is hindered not fostered.
3 At the heart of oral work in the classroom is groupwork. Class discussion has its place, but pairs or small groups of pupils are more likely to generate language that takes things and people forward.
4 Groupwork should figure large in classrooms: children should work in a variety of differently composed groups. They should make decisions and predict outcomes together, always about issues that matter and in contexts that are as real as possible.
5 As part of the process of developing language, children should be encouraged to talk about talk: to be aware of their own contribution to the group, to recognize the importance of the contribution which enables the group to progress, or which synthesizes and clarifies the group's thinking. An awareness of what causes inhibition or silence in a group should be developed. The use of cassette recorders is important in this respect.
6 Listening and talking are talents that develop naturally before children go to school. Young children asking real questions fill homes with sound. Teachers need to foster that natural growth. We listen when there is something worth hearing. Activities that accentuate speaking, but not listening, or vice versa, act against the logic that draws the two together.
7 Children benefit from being given the 'mantle of the expert', that is in being

TALKING IN GROUPS

A lot of the work you do in English involves talking. Talking about things your English teacher asks you to talk about in a group can be a lot better if you think about the following points; they can help you be a much better talker.

STARTING OFF

Talking has to start somewhere; to get going join in, ask questions and if no one is saying anything, be prepared to say something, this keeps the talk going.

LISTENING AND ENCOURAGING

If someone is talking, look at them and encourage them to feel at ease by listening carefully. You will often nod and smile at the talker without knowing it when you are listening. This makes the talker feel safe when talking because the talker knows that listening. If you do this, you will you are really listening. If you start talking, be listened to when you start talking.

If you have been listening carefully, you can carry on the talk quite easily by adding to what has been said.

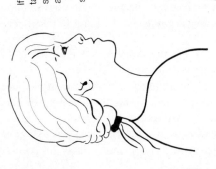

DOMINATING

If you try and dominate the talk by not giving others a chance to say anything, this stops others from talking and they won't want to talk as a result. The idea of talk is to give everyone a fair chance to say what they feel they want to say.

Remember, it is possible to get others to listen to your view without raising your voice and forcing them to listen. Try and persuade others by saying what you have to say clearly and calmly; there's no need to shout!

CARRYING ON AND KEEPING GOING

If you feel the talk is leading away from what you should be talking about, don't be afraid to lead the talk back to what you talking about. This can be done without being rude and will be accepted by the group.

If, however, you completely change the subject all of a sudden, this can damage the talk that has been going on.

SILENCES

Not everyone finds talking in groups easy and people accept that others may be quiet, but if you say nothing in a group this will be unhelpful and this will bother the people in the group who are talking. Even if you are shy (and many are!) it's best to join in a little. If you have listened carefully to others, they will listen to you.

Also, if someone is saying very little, you can help them by asking them what they think.

JOINING IN

The best talk happens when everyone listens as well as joining in. By in a group listens in what you talk about and everyone joining in what might be decided is everyone's work and not just the work of the few.

FINALLY

Now try them out – see if these tips do work. Don't be surprised if they do!

Figure 2.9 Talking tips

asked to explain a process, an issue, a passion about which they may know more than the teacher. The teacher who can play the role of 'the knowing innocent' can liberate such talk.

8 Story is a powerful force in our lives and pupils of all ages should experience that power regularly. Teachers should tell and read stories and encourage our natural fascination for narrative, for personal anecdote, for the way life unfolds. Such an emphasis on story can build confidence in pupils' ability to talk at length and hold an audience.

A note on self-assessment

Included here is a document produced by a group of teachers to help pupils look critically at their own oral work (Figure 2.9).[31] The pupils' comments are disconcertingly searching:

> I think I was quite good in the discussion. I said my views and my points, I didn't shout or argue or butt in. Maybe I could have put more expression into it and questioned some people to make it sound better.

> I wish that I could have said more, but I also thought it's fair that the others, like the more shy people, would get a chance to speak or even persuade them to speak. I would say that others did quite well, I suppose all of us could have done even better, but this type of work can be very difficult. If work like this goes on, I feel that it is worth joining into.

3 Writing

Sir, I Ham a very Bad Hand at Righting.

Tidd, Cato Street Conspirator,
quoted by Tony Harrison in 'On Not Being Milton'.[1]

Teachers provide the greatest encouragement for children to communicate in writing when they respond more to the content of what is written than to errors, and when they share a child's writing with other children.

(*English for Ages 5 to 16*, 17.12)

In the first draft of the opening of this section I wrote boldly, 'Writing is difficult for most of us . . .'; but then paused, reflected anxiously on my own difficulty – and went to lunch! Its difficulty for children is evident throughout the years of formal schooling; it can elicit groans, resentment and pain:

> For many children, writing is that aspect of language which yields the least reward and the most potential for failure, while for teachers it can become the means through which children are assessed, rather than the opportunity to extend horizons.

'Writing', said one of the pupils asked about attitudes to writing in the early stages of The National Writing Project, 'gives me a pain in the head. I'm giving up the writing and going on to the reading!' It is not just pupils who suffer; teachers, too, sometimes fret over what they and their pupils are going through.

Yet writing is powerful and important: both qualities recognized by those nineteenth-century do-gooders who attempted to 'kill the language'[2] by restricting those who had access to the written word. 'I allow of no writing for the poor', said Hannah More in 1834, and such blind certainty persisted deep into the century, fostered by Methodist ministers and others: 'I remember hearing a clergyman oppose educating the people on the grounds that they would write nasty things on the walls.'[3] This is hard to imagine when so much paper is covered now with Biro and pencil – too much probably. Donald Graves opens his important book on the teaching of writing thus:

> Children want to write. They want to write the first day they attend school. This is no accident. Before they went to school they marked up walls, pavements,

newspapers with crayons, chalk, pens or pencils . . . anything that makes a mark. The child's marks say, 'I am'. 'No, you aren't', say most school approaches to the teaching of writing.[4]

When children write for real purposes and for a real audience, the importance of writing can be understood by all children. But the ghosts of shady practice still swirl as Gareth Owen reminds us in his wickedly funny poem, 'Miss Creedle Teaches Creative Writing':

Are we ready to imagine Darren?
I'm going to count to three.
At one, we wipe our brains completely clean;
At two, we close our eyes;
And at three, we imagine.[5]

Both Gareth Owen's poem and the following telling dialogue written by Andrew Stibbs, are effective ways of opening a staff discussion about writing.

If we taught kids to speak like we teach them to write . . .

Kid [in kitchen]: Mummy, Mummy [pause] Mummy, Mummy!
Mum [in next room]: Don't repeat yourself, dear.
K: A big cat's just comed in the window.
M: Grammar!
K: Now puss on stove.
M: Don't use slang. The word is 'cat'.
K: Now cat in frying pan.
M: Good!
K: Fish comed out of pan.
M: What's the good of my correcting your speech if you take no notice?
K: Pan falled over. Fire in pan.
M: Not a sentence.
K: Now fire in hanged-up clothes by chimbly.
M: Pronunciation! The word is 'chimney'. Say it out ten times.
K: Chimney, chimney, chimby, chimly, chimbly . . . Now fire in granny!
M: Try to vary the shape of your sentences.
K: Now granny in fire.
M: Better! But make your speech more interesting by using more describing words.
K: See how the pretty yellow flames lick round the frail and combustible granny, like the greedy, angry tongues of hungry tigers, which seem . . . AAAR-RRGGGHHH!!!
M: Why is this sentence not finished? Five out of ten.

How teachers 'set up' writing tasks and how they respond to them, and when, are crucial and danger-strewn questions. The lessons of Miss Creedle's chastening demands and the rigorous criticism of Mum in our second example shouldn't be ignored: overweening adults can kill off language – or writing anyway – as readily as nineteenth-century zealots!

Figure 3.1   Selection of statements about writing[6]

Many secondary schools require a great deal of copying from the blackboard, particularly in subjects with a high information content, and yet many junior schools require children to do very little copying from the blackboard. Again, we should like to see a little movement on each side, each towards the other. For the sake of children's practice, if only in preparation for the transfer, junior schools might do more work which requires copying from the blackboard. Secondary schools should ensure that (i) children are introduced carefully to the practice, (ii) blackboard work is understandable in its format and legible in its writing and (iii) copying from the blackboard is only part of the total writing demand   (A)

Successful writing will often be displayed, at times in magazines, about the school, in the library so that other pupils may share it. It might be read out, discussed by other children and suggestions made for improvement.   (B)

In order to write imaginatively the child must have something to write about, a wealth of words with which to express his ideas, the tool of handwriting, the opportunity to write when he feels creative, and time to finish his work.

In these few lines Alice Yardley expresses the needs of the young child in the simplest terms. She gives priority to *something to write about,* and this is the very heart of the matter. Only in providing the freshness of first-hand experiences, as an incentive to writing, can teachers expect children to use language which has sincerity and vitality. This may be one answer to the question, *'Why write?'* By this kind of expressive writing children can clarify their own imaginative thinking and share it with others.   (C)

What does seem crucial is for the children themselves to be involved at every stage. This includes deciding what to do and why, as well as planning activities. It is vital for children not to have these important stages taken over and done for them by their teacher!   (D)

As the 1982 primary Report has it, 'The wholly laudable aims of neatness and correctness are easily exaggerated in their own right to the exclusion of *greater expectations of success* in writing (emphasis added). It is arguable that the work of numbers of 11 year olds in the middle band of performance could be improved by a more specific awareness of various types of writing rather than having their minds concentrated on a narrow range of mainly surface features common to writing as a whole.'   (E)

What is the process we should teach? It is the process of discovery through language. It is the process of exploration of what we know and what we feel about what we know through language. It is the process of using language to learn about our world, to evaluate what we learn about our world to communicate what we learn about our world.

Instead of teaching finished writing, we should teach unfinished writing and glory in its unfinishedness. We work with language in action. We share with our students the continual excitement of choosing one word instead of another, of searching for the one true word.

This is not a question of correct or incorrect, of etiquette or custom. This is a matter of far higher importance. The writer, as he writes, is making ethical decisions. He doesn't test his words by a rule book, but by life. He uses language to reveal the truth to himself so that he can tell it to others. It is an exciting, eventful, evolving process.

This process of discovery through language we call writing can be introduced to your classroom as soon as you have a very simple understanding of that process, and as soon as you accept the full implications of that process, and as soon as you accept the full implications of teaching process, not product.   (F)

Figure 3.1—continued

Real writing is purposeful communication by writers to their readers. Real writers are those involved in writing for the purpose of communicating their own thoughts and/or feelings to their readers, which may include themselves
(G)

In particular, teachers should protect themselves and children from the disabling consequences of evaluation. Where evaluation and grading are unavoidable, as they so often are, it can be made clear to children that the 'mark' is given for administrative or bureaucratic purposes that have nothing to do with 'real world' writing. Grading never taught a writer anything (except that he or she was not a member of the club). Writers learn by learning about writing, not by getting letters or numbers put on their efforts and abilities. Children (and university students) who will write only for a grade have learnt an odd notion of the advantages of the club of writers.

This is not a question of 'correction', which in any case does not make anyone a better writer. Correction merely highlights what learners almost certainly know they cannot do in the first place. Correction is worthwhile only if the learner would seek it in any case, and to seek correction you must regard yourself as a professional, an established member of the club. I am not saying there should not be standards, but that the standards have to come from what the learner wants and expects to achieve. Emphasis on the suppression of errors results in the suppression of writing.   (H)

The teaching of two of the three Rs – reading and writing – will revert to the best of tried and true principles of thirty years ago if recommendations by the Government's school inspectors are adopted. They want children to receive more teaching of the rudiments of grammar, punctuation and spelling, how to speak and express themselves properly.   (I)

By the age of 7 all children should have had experiences of writing and teaching designed to develop their confidence as young writers and to assist them in finding purpose and pleasure in the process of writing. They should be helped towards an implicit understanding that the written word differs sharply from the spoken in its procedures, conventions and demands. It should be an objective for the work of all children that close links be established between experience (both direct and indirect) and writing and that talk and reading should be customary preliminaries (and/or accompaniments) to writing. It would also be appropriate that various forms of narrative should feature most prominently and might embrace at least:
● accounts of experiences
● the writing of stories
● accounts of something the pupils have learned or read about or of learning activities in which they have taken part.   (J)

All children should also have had extensive experience of planned intervention and support, in accordance with their individual needs and related to appropriate tasks and contexts, with regard to the development of their writing skills. In general these will encompass: handwriting, spelling, punctuation, the development of sentence variety, control and organization, paragraphing, and the proof-reading, editing and re-drafting of some of their own work.

Most children at this age might be assisted to begin to take some explicit account of the need to vary their writing according to specific purposes, contexts and readerships
(K)

As to writing, the aims should be to enable pupils:
● to write for a range or purposes
● to organize the content of what is written in ways appropriate to the purposes
● to use styles of writing appropriate to the purposes and the intended readership
● to use spelling, punctuation and syntax accurately and with confidence.   (L)

A policy for writing

As the language post-holder, where do you begin in a new appointment if the school's policy for writing has been lost, or has faded in the sun? Here are some possibilities; what order of priority would you decide upon?

- Write a policy statement. Put it into everyone's pigeon-hole.
- Mug up on Donald Graves, Frank Smith and so on and write a discussion paper for a staff meeting.
- Ask someone else to sort out a writing policy.
- Find out what's happening in the classroom.
- Go to the pub.
- Ask local employers or secondary schools what kind of writing they need.
- Go on a course.
- Get an 'expert' in to talk to the staff about an aspect of writing.
- Discuss as a team what kinds of writing children need.
- Map the demands of the National Curriculum Programmes of Study.
- Any others?

That, in a sense, is the easy part: the likelihood is that there will be a degree of consensus about the more sensible courses of action. While going to the pub has its attractions (!), we would suggest that 'Find out what's happening in the classroom' and 'Discuss as a team what kinds of writing children need' *in the light of the National Curriculum* should figure fairly high if the policy is going to work and be appropriate.

WHAT SHOULD THE POLICY SAY?

At the heart of any policy should be a clear vision of what writing is. Figure 3.1 is a selection of statements about writing:

1 On your own, select one that sums up Writing for you: the one voice that strikes the most powerful chord.
2 Discuss that with another member of staff.
3 Underline all those elements that should figure in your school's language policy.
4 Compare these statements with the demands of the National Curriculum at KS1 and KS2. Are there any shifts in emphasis or issues which remain neglected?

A real community of readers and writers[7]

Read the child's writing in Figure 3.2. Under what circumstances was it written? How old was the writer? For whom was it written? What do you think of it as a teacher and as a reader? Where did the writing come from?

My Dad running in the ½ marathon | – 10-83
My Dad went running in the ½ marathon. He
was going with his friends Chris and Davied.
So they came round to are house in there
Car's with there familys So when they came
We Set of.
        We Soon got there We parKed the Car
and got Out and walKeddoWn the hill. The
race was about to Start.
        We Saw Daddy running With one of his
friends Tony after We had Seen him run
We Went to get Our Lunch. We a te. t under
a tree then We got down to the race again.
The first peaple Were Comming up.
        first We Saw Stuart Tony's friend then
We Saw Chris then tony then at last my
Dad Came I Clapped till my hands ach
-ed and I Shouted as if I never could
agian. I Went to See my Dad at the
finish there he was he was Wearing a
lovely gold medle my I felt proud of
him I relly did!
                THE END

Figure 3.2   Child's piece of writing

In some ways the last of those questions is the most significant: Abby wrote the way she did at the age of 8 because she had absorbed the style of a developing story from what she had read and what had been read to her; not only that, she had a story to tell and an emotion to explore. It is not, it should be said, a piece written in school! It was written within the hour of returning from the Half Marathon, for herself – and then for her family. In that sense, it is a very 'real' piece of writing.

When children write in school, it is not always easy to replicate Abby's apparent enjoyment in the process. But unless the school's writing policy is explicit and the subject of constant scrutiny and debate, children can learn too many false lessons and bad habits.

SOME QUESTIONS ABOUT WRITING

- Was the original stimulus for writing strong enough?
- Is it realistic to expect the class to write on a common theme and for a common purpose?
- Are there enough opportunities for children to write for an audience other than a red-pen-toting teacher?
- Are the children aware of the purpose of the writing?
- Are they aware of the difference in language necessary for different audiences?
- Is there an element of 'contract' in the writing, or does the teacher insist on the topic, approach and consequences?
- Is work ever published?
- Does the redrafting go beyond 'manicuring the corpse'?[8]
- How do you react when the children ask, 'How much must we write?'
- In looking for development in writing, what do we mean?
- Is writing ever used as a punishment? If so, what does that say to the children about writing?
- At what point and by what methods should the children be acquainted with the importance of skills like spelling, syntax and so on?
- Do the children ever just write for themselves?
- Is writing seen as a craft? Do you write?!
- Is the process valued as much as the product?

These questions raise many issues: about the purpose of writing; about the response to it; about the craft and process of writing. Figure 3.3. is intended to sharpen that focus.

TWENTY-ONE WAYS TO DISCOURAGE GOOD WRITING!

Martin Coles[9] responded in *Education* magazine to *English from 5 to 16* in a wry and telling fashion: 'In this spirit of encouraging practices which have a negative effect on the development of children's writing I offer the following advice'. What follows is a series of spoof epigrams about writing, on 'response', for example: 'Make sure that all writing is given a mark out of ten, but never give anyone 10/10. That child will obviously not be encouraged to do better.' On drafting, his mock 'advice' is clear:

> Make sure a child knows that his writing must be right first time. Never allow a child to alter what he has written. It is possible of course for a child to reflect on what he has written, to change or erase words, to revise the order of things, to add thoughts, but this only wastes time that could be used to do more important things, like learning about the functions and names of all the main parts of speech.

Figure 3.3 'A real community of readers and writers'

WRITING AS POWER	'Unfortunately the powers above soon noticed that . . . education was not necessarily at all to the employer's advantage . . . it was decided that after all it was wicked to teach poor children to write.'[10]	Real writing belongs to the writer. *What writing tasks help children's developing language?*
WRITING AND DEVELOPMENT	'In children's writing we need to look for what the writing does for the writer.'[11]	Development is 'spiral', not linear. *How can children become aware of their own development as writers?*
WRITING AND ASSESSMENT	'I acquired my formal marking style along with my PGCE . . . became an expert in the field of red pens. No medieval monk lavished more care on his marginalia than I did during my first months.'[12]	Response! Comments should be (i) text-specific and (ii) help to push the pupil on. *How much scope is there for self-assessment?*
WRITING FOR LEARNING	'The whole point of being a writer, it seems to me, is that you change as you write, you change yourself, you change the way you think.'[13]	'What do I already know? → Things I'd like to know → How do I find out? → Exploration → Have I found out what I wanted to know? *When should writing contribute to learning?*
WRITING AS PROCESS	' "Destructive writing's what I need", growled Trish. "Every letter a bullet . . ." '[14]	*Should the* **process** *be valued as much as the* **product***?*
CRAFTING, DRAFTING AND WRITING	'We have all heard the groan in the classrooms, "Do I have to copy it over?" This is the popular understanding of revision. Put a good manicure on the corpse.'[15]	Composing → Revising → Editing → Publishing *Who decides?*

Figure 3.3—continued

WRITING AND THE TEACHER	'If teachers set writing as punishment, what message about writing does that give the children?'	Demonstrate it! *How do you help a child through a piece of writing?*
STARTING WRITING	'Teachers don't teach you to write: they just tell you to do it.'[16]	*What are the best ways of getting children started on a piece of writing?*
WHAT FEEDS WRITING?	'Reading and writing should float on a sea of talk.'[17]	*What kinds of talk and reading?*
WHAT KINDS OF WRITING?	' "Miss Beale said you would show me round, to look at the projects", said Andrew. "Why, do you want to copy one?" asked Victor.'[18]	*What kinds of writing do your children like most?*
WRITING AND THE WORDPROCESSOR	'I have seen a child move from total rejection of writing to an intense involvement . . . within a few weeks.'[19]	Automatic Tippex. *Which wordprocessor and why?*
WRITING AND AUDIENCE	'We believe children should write for a purpose. What better purpose is there than publishing a book?'[20]	Range of audience and publishing. *How does the teacher's role change when the audience is real?*
QUESTIONS FOR A TERM'S WORK	FIND OUT: 1 How many different kinds of real audience 'work'. 2 What the ideal classroom organization for writing is. 3 What the wordprocessor can do for writing. 4 What impact can a diet of 'real' books have on writing. 5 What children think about writing. 6 What different kinds of writing can be done in, say, science.	

Both 'drafting' and 'response' to writing are difficult areas, principally because, in both, the essence of success depends upon the teacher's intervention: knowing how and when to push the child on. Development in writing depends upon motivation in the child, a teacher with an eye for context, audience and purpose, as well as someone who knows how to guide, prompt, encourage or lie low.

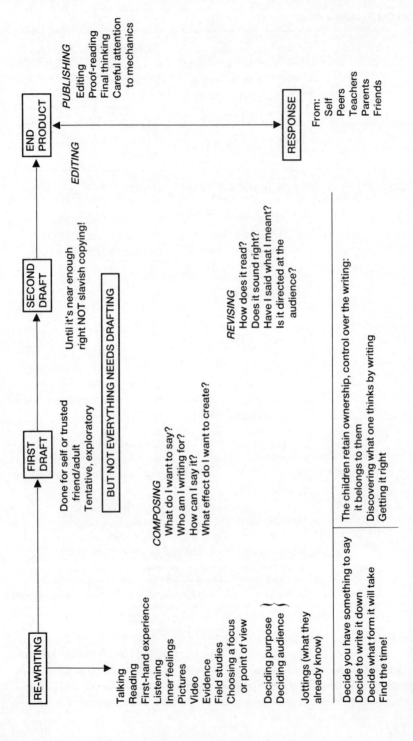

Figure 3.4 Developing writing

Drafting

Figure 3.4 maps the process of writing from the initial stages to the point of publication and subsequent response.[21] It is a useful exercise to 'overlay' specific programmes of work on this map and discuss the teacher's role throughout the activity.

Responding to writing

At other points in this book emphasis is placed on the children themselves being involved in the process of evaluating their own language work. Many teachers have found the use of 'response partnerships' beneficial. The strategy outlined below was suggested to us by Pat D'Arcy.[22] The partnership will involve two, perhaps three, pupils; these are their 'instructions':

1 Have the writer read out loud what she or he has written so far.
2 Listen carefully while the reading aloud is taking place. Don't interrupt.
3 When the reading aloud is finished *don't* try to comment immediately. Take about five minutes (the writer as well as the listeners) to jot down whatever most sticks in your mind from what you have just heard (about the events or the scene or the issues or whatever).
4 Take it in turns to read out what you have jotted down.
5 Let the writer explain what she or he is pleased with so far; also what she/he is having problems with and how she/he sees the piece developing.
6 Discuss any of these points with the writer.

Case study 1: reasons for writing

The table of results (Figure 3.5) is from a survey carried out in my own school, into the purpose for which children write. (Obviously, this doesn't include 'school-induced' writing or homework.) All of the itemized 'reasons for writing' were drawn from the children, with no prompting from me other than 'What else do you write for/What other things do you use writing for when you're not at school?'

The categorization into 'Personal Interest' and 'Functional Writing' is my own, not the children's. Inevitably there are areas of overlap: 'Recipes', for example, could belong to either, or both, categories.

Each 'reason' given was written on the blackboard (the children themselves were not required to write anything), followed by a show of hands from those whoever 'did' the item in question. (Frequency of writing for any particular item was not taken into account.)

The sample consisted of between 130 and 150 children over the age range 7 to 11+, drawn from a mainly skilled, working-class and professional catchment area.

Although the research design is too loose, and the sample too limited in size and range of population-type for drawing any major conclusions, the results do, nevertheless, show some interesting features and trends across the age-range. To me the most notable feature was the amazingly wide variety of purposes for writing (and, therefore, styles of writing used) by children at the end of their primary education.

WHY DO CHILDREN WRITE?

Type of writing	Class's responses as a %				
	IT	2S*	2W	3R	4V
A. *Personal interest*					
Stories		60	60	43	69
Poems		44			50
Songs				10	
Letters (other than 'Thank you')	73	60	48	60	81
Cards – birthday	100	80	100	100	100
– Christmas	96		100	100	100
– invitations	92		84	90	100
– holiday	77	60	76	80	100
'Fun cards'	77				
Chain letters	35		16		
Recalling school events		32			
Hobbies and interests		12	40	43	62
Secret codes			76		
Recipes			48		
B. *Functional writing*					
'Thank you' letters	88	40	72	100	100
Father Christmas letters	88		20		
Tooth-Fairy letters	50		8		
Lists – shopping	54	36	36	43	62
– present				87	88
Practising handwriting		32	40		
Forms – competition		32	80	60	} 73
– application/membership				60	
Labelling – own name			60		
– information with drawings/ diagrams			48	57	65
Keeping scores		} 80	44	} 77	54
Games and quizzes (other than scoring)			84		65
Phone numbers and addresses			48		96
Messages for other people					77
Notes on calendar or diary			20		81
Memos to self			40		58
Accounts (pocket money)					73
Writing directions (e.g. to a place)					46
Writing instructions/rules (e.g. for a game)					35
Cataloguing information/storage systems			24		38

*2S is a mixed class – first and second years.

Figure 3.5   Table of results from Case study 1

If nothing else, it has helped the children to realize that writing is no longer merely a school-based task, but an essential, useful and pleasurable activity which has evolved from within their own world.[23]

Case study 2: journals, think books, learning logs

I wanted to give children the opportunity to write for themselves, not just for me. Hence, the Learning Log!

I began these logs with my class of 9–11 year olds with varying degrees of success. The children used them in differing ways, some using them as diaries, some to relate problems, some to plan work and record ideas. For some children they have been a great success, giving them choice and freedom in their writing. The less able, however, have not yet chosen to write readily in their logs and I feel that I need to devote more time to helping these children gain more joy from writing.

I feel that I have gained a greater understanding of the children through their logs and this has helped build relationships with a group of difficult children. My comments, though time-consuming, have been eagerly received by my writers. It has also encouraged me to be less superficial in my comments; I pay greater attention now to developing the children's writing.[24]

Case study 3: writing and the word processor

The machine has a magic and this new writing is a pleasure. It may not create genius but it helps the common scribe to enjoy toil.[25]

I've been keen to prevent the micro being regarded as at the edge of what we do, you know that Seymour Papert remark,[26] what is it, about the micro being one of the trendy gadgets 'to teach the same old stuff in thinly disguised versions of the same old way'? I like that. I'm glad to say that the micro is now an accepted and central part of the writing process for my class . . .

We use two different WP packages, both chips, EDWORD and WORDWISE PLUS – the choice was more a matter of chance than logic. I felt a glimmer of confidence with WORDWISE, having taken the computer home one weekend and played with it long enough to stem the panic. Of course, I shouldn't have worried since the kids have a more blasé view of the world, invariably assuming that the machine will work, while my assumption was infinitely more pessimistic! What struck me most was the fact that kids who usually found writing a struggle were the ones who were most keen to exploit the computer for all it was worth. They liked the instant obliteration of errors, the sliding of their words across the screen, the chattering print-out of perfect copy.

Interestingly, a number of significant changes have happened since then. These are less to do with computers and more to do with how children and staff regard writing. There is more genuine drafting, more discussion, more collaboration and sharing. We publish more often, more effectively and for audiences other than me.

We have also made good use of Quinkey – if you don't know it, it's a small word processor operated by using the five keys on a hand-sized keyboard. Adults learning the appropriate sequence of keys to be pressed to form letters and words seem to be reduced to fuming incompetence, but the children learn fast enough. Our early work with Quinkey uses QUAD, which splits the screen into four quarters, each of which is controlled by one child of a group of four. The children are very motivated and 'teach' each other and themselves – our teachers are thus freer to give time elsewhere. It is of real importance to us that Quinkey maximizes the use of a computer since so many children can genuinely participate.

Case study 4: pupil power – language, the media and modern technology[27]

We set out to make a video[28] about Microcomputers and English, but what emerged was, in a sense, more far reaching than that . . .

Twenty-eight 9 and 10 year olds[29] were involved in a project intended to acquaint them with microtechnology through simulating, as realistically as possible, the processing of news in a busy newsroom. The children had very little experience of computers at the outset and what they learned was not the result of teacher direction, but stemmed from real needs and real use as the project unfolded.

The aims of the project were, I suppose, ambitious: we wanted the pupils to learn how news comes into the home; how a newspaper is made; how radio and TV news works; about teletext, about computers; that what comes out of a computer is only the product of someone else's input. The children would use a video camera. They'd learn that news was constantly changing; that it can be manipulated and it isn't always true; that presentation varies with audience. Surrounding all this was an expectation that children can benefit from working under a shared pressure, that cooperation matters and so do deadlines!

We split the class into four groups, each of which worked in one area of the media. In all, I suppose, each group had about six hours of preparation before 'the event'; these included visits to the *Slough Observer* newspaper and Radio 210. A proportion of time was spent on familiarizing the children with the technology. Later we introduced some outlines of news stories which they extended and developed.

A crucial element in the next phase was the program EXTRA,[30] which very realistically simulates the flow of news coming into a newsroom: the realism extends to a warning alarm when a story is about to break – 'Message on Line' – followed by an urgent chatter of print-out. An account of a lion escaping from the nearby Windsor Safari Park broke in that way.

The school had cleared a day to enable the project to draw to a climax. The children came into the 'newsroom', expecting to finalize the stories they had for imminent publication. What they were not expecting was the story that started coming off the printer: at about 5 to 11 they had the first indication that a bomb had exploded in Hyde Park. It meant, of course, urgent adaptation of front pages and broadcasts!

Throughout the project the children were absorbed in the work, but the context for writing (and talk) became so real during the day that the bustle of the newsroom and the approaching deadline caught us all.

Children wrote and talked with enthusiasm, as well as a clearly defined sense of purpose. It was also a salutary lesson for us about what children of 9 and 10 can achieve. The video, we feel, should be compulsory viewing for every teacher in the neighbouring comprehensive![31]

'The micro is not a threat to writing. It is a liberating influence, a powerful tool, a starting point for new ways of using language. . .'[32]

Planning writing activities

My own recommendations for how writing and reading should be taught are perhaps radical; they should not be taught at all. Not in any formal sense, as *subjects*. All the busywork, the meaningless drills and exercises, the rote memorization, the irrelevant tests, and the distracting grades should go . . . in their place teachers and children together should use writing (and reading, spoken language, art and drama) to learn other things. . . .

Children should learn to write in the same manner that they learn to talk, without being aware that they are doing so, in the course of doing other things.[33]

	Agree	*Don't agree*	*Don't know*
Boys are better writers than girls.			
Stories are easy to write.			
Writing is the most important thing we do in school.			
Writing poems is fun.			
Writing neatly matters a lot.			
Silence is best for writing.			
You have to be clever to write well.			
Teachers should correct all mistakes.			
It's silly to write about things which can't really happen.			
Starting a piece of writing is the hardest thing.			
The longer the writing the better it is.			
Talking to a friend helps you write.			
Bad spelling spoils writing.			
The best stories have happy endings.			
It's easy to write about things you can see.			
You need to make mistakes to learn to write.			

Figure 3.6   Children's questionnaire about writing[34]

It is necessary to plan writing activities with great sensitivity: there's a lot to remember in terms of our intentions and expectations, as well as the pupils' perceptions, certainties and fears. Figure 3.6 is a valuable source of information about the latter: group discussion and responses to the questionnaire will provide some interesting pointers to the customers' view of the school's writing policy. If, as in one school, over half the children believe that teachers should correct all mistakes, or that 'silence is best for writing', it raises questions about which the staff need to talk. In our sample, too, just over 30 per cent felt that 'You have to be clever to write well'; more significantly, though, nearly a quarter of the children didn't know the answer to that question whereas on other issues, most of them had very clear opinions.

Looking back over a sequence of work, and reflecting upon the opportunities and audiences the children have been provided with, is a good habit – especially if you do it with a friend or colleague. Using a prompt like the one in Figure 3.7 adds a rigour to the activity.[35]

Activity	Audience						
USING INFORMATION	Self	Teacher	Other adult	Younger child	Peer	Older child	Other (Specify)
Recording Reporting Explaining Instructing Speculating Persuading/Arguing							
PERSONAL WRITING Autobiography Responses Imaginative narrative							
EXPERIMENTAL WRITING Verse, poetry Playscripts Journals, diaries Think books							
ANY OTHERS!							

Figure 3.7   Looking at writing

Twenty-one ways to encourage writing

1 Write with the children sometimes.
2 Try out new starting points for writing.
3 Promote discussion during the writing process.
4 Encourage journal writing.
5 Think about creating the right environment.

6 Respond, don't just 'mark'.
7 Allow more time for reflective writing.
8 Encourage drafting when it's appropriate.
9 Read more fiction and poetry.
10 Use the 'Writers of Schools' scheme.
11 Encourage a wide range of writing activities.
12 Look for other, real audiences.
13 Involve children in self-assessment.
14 Beware of too much writing.
15 Encourage 'response partnerships'.
16 Value 'creation at the point of utterance'.
17 Be sceptical of 'exercises'.
18 Publish; make books; display the work.
19 Raise the children's awareness of what writing is and can be.
20 Exploit children's fascination with story.
21 Talk about writing.

The trappings of writing surround children in school: pens, paper, chalk, blackboards, wordprocessors. It is high profile and, perhaps, too high in status: talk, all too readily, is relegated in importance. Talk – sounds in the air – is ephemeral, intangible, despite the cassette recorder. Writing, too, however, is an indicator of thought; it can be written for oneself as well as for an audience; it should be protected from association with drudgery and punishment, the mechanical and the aimless.

> On the blackboard she'd pinned a picture of a fishing boat in difficulties. . .
>
> 'Careful, beautiful copying please . . . don't rush . . . it's so easy to make a mistake when you're thinking about your handwriting. Good! . . . Who's got an idea for the next sentence?'
>
> Godfrey yawned elaborately.

In Chris Powling's excellent short story 'An Oscar for Godfrey', from which the extract above is taken,[36] both young Godfrey and his teacher, Miss Dixon demonstrate great wit, insight and intelligence. For all that, neither of them bring those qualities to the classroom's writing activities! The art in 'teaching writing' lies there: beguiling the pupil with the power and possibilities that can flow from the pen.

Spelling (AT4)

Attainment Target 4 (which refers only to Levels 1 and 4) is recognized as being distinct from the other aspects of writing by those who drafted the National Curriculum. As is pointed out in *English for Ages 5 to 16*:

> if both composing and secretarial abilities were included in one global writing attainment target a pupil who had achieved Level 6 in the composing aspect but only Level 3 in the secretarial aspect would have to be recorded as being at Level 3 in writing.

Contrary to some popular views teachers continue to give a good deal of attention to the teaching of spelling. The most common strategy is the 'Look Cover Write Check' (LCWC) method which recognizes that the solutions to spelling difficulties need to be tailored to the needs of individual pupils.

The LCWC approach concentrates only on the child's visual memory but it is also important that she or he learns how the word sounds. Sensibly some teachers insert the word 'say' after 'look'.

It is sometimes a good idea to ask parents to help with their child's spelling (as long as it doesn't become a chore!). It might also be useful to give out a brief outline of the approach like the one shown opposite.[37]

A number of fairly common types of spelling errors have been identified[38] which help teachers to match the right approach to the specific difficulty:

- Mispronunciation
- Over applying a rule (e.g. runned for ran)
- Word shortening
- Letter reversal
- Consonants (doubling or not)
- Reversing letters
- Confusing words that sound the same (homophones)
- Missing out silent letters
- Morphological errors (ignoring the changes in word structure, e.g. suffixes and prefixes, etc.)
- Are there any others that you've encountered?

Finally

Writing is increasingly recognized as a means of communication which is more effectively used where there is a proper stimulus, clear definition of purpose and a recognized audience.

HMI[39]

4 Reading for meaning, for pleasure and for life

Good reader

My little brother's reading really well.
He brings his words home in a little tin
and he can pick out aeroplane
from Pat and Peter, dog and Jane.

Oh yes, my brother's reading really well.
He named his rabbits John and Janet,
then Dick and Dora. Now they're Nip and Fluff.
He tries to keep up with the latest stuff.

His teacher says he's reading really well.
He knows this string of words by heart: tree little
milk egg book school sit frog . . . He scores the best
marks in his class on every reading test.

It's plain to see he's reading really well.
Yesterday he stopped the talk at breakfast
by asking, can the rat pat the fat cat?
My dad didn't know what to make of that.

He said he'd cancel all my brother's comics,
but Mum said it was all the fault of phonics.
He'd soon be back to normal and besides
the clever lad was reading really well.

Ask him what he's reading and immediately
he'll tell you he's on Level 4, Book 3 –
same as last month. He must like that book a lot.
I'm glad my brother's reading really well.

Our Grandma thought that he might like a book
at Christmas, but she had the sense to look
into his room and found one there already.
Oh yes, she said, he's reading really well.

She bought him an electric train instead
and now his book is opened up – not read.
It makes a lovely tunnel for the train.
It's lucky that he's reading really well.

Barrie Wade[1]

I am for getting a boy forward with his reading, for that is a sure good. I would let him at first read any English book which happens to engage his attention, because you have done a great deal when you have brought him to have entertainment from a book.

Samuel Johnson

Reading is arguably the most sensitive area of the language co-ordinator's responsibilities – and not just for boys! On appointment to a new school, or on promotion, it is not unusual for a headteacher to ask the post-holder to 'look at the reading scheme'. Reading is a high-status area. Parents are concerned (justifiably) about their child's progress in reading: they recognize that it gives access to a wide range of areas of learning. Unofficially, LEAs may even judge the effectiveness of a school on data drawn from reading tests applied across the Authority. However, it should be remembered that these so-called 'objective' reading tests have only limited shelf lives and the greater the time interval over which they are applied, the less certain it can be that the school populations which are tested are comparable.

All teachers are teachers of reading, and the vast majority, whatever their experience, will have a view on reading. Consequently, it is important for the language co-ordinator to be equipped to respond in an informed way to queries from parents and colleagues and to be able to counter prejudice, myths or misunderstanding about the reading process. This is all the more important at a time when there has been little in the way of closely reasoned argument about reading and rather too much ill-informed assertion.

Some of the more energetic exchanges in both the professional and popular press have been concerned with the relative merits of the so-called 'real book' approach to reading and other strategies which depend predominantly on the teaching of phonics. In many ways this part of the 'reading debate' has been the least fruitful. In the *HMI Review of the Year – Standards in Education 1989/90*, the then Senior Chief Inspector said that:

> Primary teachers take reading seriously. There is no evidence of a Gaderene rush into real books teaching methods, nor indeed into an exclusive use of any one method: an approach clearly linked to poor standards of performance whatever the single method might be.

A little later in the same document the then chief HMI goes on to say:

> Poor work is not strongly associated with any particular method of teaching reading. It appears to have much more to do with inadequate planning, unsound management and organisation of the teaching and learning, inconsistencies in applying teaching methods and poor assessment of children's progress.

Interestingly the HMI report *The Teaching and Learning of Reading in Primary Schools* which was published in January 1991, went some way towards exploding some of the myths about reading:

- In schools where pupils demonstrated poor reading performance it was interesting that there had also been high teacher turnover in the past three years.
- Only about 5 per cent of teachers used a real books approach exclusively.
- Only 3 per cent of teachers used a phonics approach exclusively.
- In 95 per cent of the classes HMI visited published graded reading schemes were in place and were being used.
- In almost all of the schools visited phonic skills were being taught, usually to some good effect.
- The vast majority of teachers use a mixture of teaching methods.
- Primary school teachers give an extremely high priority to teaching children to read in Key Stage 1.
- HMI also noted that there had not been a fall in the overall standards of reading in primary schools since their primary survey of 1978.

The Language and Literacy team at the University of Brighton have written that skilled reading:

> requires the ability to know when to use a knowledge of language structure, the world we live in, and the correspondences between marks on the page and sounds in our head, to make sense of texts, and to orchestrate all these to make connections between texts and kinds of texts so that each reading experience makes its contribution to the meanings that will be possible when we pick up the next piece of reading matter.

Clearly it is also extremely important that the approach to reading decided upon by a school is consistent with the view of learning which underpins all of the work going on in that school. This book's thinking has been based on a developmental view of learning:

> It is a confusion of everyday thought that we tend to regard 'knowledge' as something that exists independently of someone who knows. 'What is known' must in fact be brought to life afresh within every 'knower' by his own efforts.[2]

This is acutely relevant to a co-ordinator's consideration of reading in that the meaning of a text does not lie on the printed page but within the mind of the reader. Reading is an active process: meaning is 'brought to life afresh' through an energetic collaboration or dialogue between the writer and the reader. Frank Smith sums this up neatly by saying that 'reading is asking questions of printed text. And reading with comprehension becomes a matter of getting your questions answered.' This is true both for the beginner and the more experienced reader. As Marie Clay has said:

> The smartest readers ask of themselves the most effective questions for reducing the uncertainty; the poorer readers bumble around with the trivial questions and

waste their opportunities to reduce uncertainty. They do not put the information-seeking process into effective sequences.

The skilled teacher orchestrates 'a range of strategies so that each individual reader has her particular needs met'.[3]

Understanding is achieved when there is an overlap between what the writer is saying in print and what the reader already knows. Comprehension, then, depends on the experience a reader brings to the text.

Case study 1: what is a reader?[4]

The first present I bought my daughter was a garishly illustrated Nursery Rhyme board book. She was a few days old. I propped the book open near her when I was changing her, or when she was lying in her pram or sitting in her bouncer. So began her introduction to the world of books which has continued unabated ever since. . .

She reads her books to herself expertly turning the pages; running her fingers under the words. She can find her way round books; she knows about indexes, contents pages and illustrations. She loves being read to, she listens attentively to taped stories and she likes it when you tell her stories. . .

We are now at a turning point it seems to me and I don't know which way to turn . . . I have a model of learning to read and the teaching of reading that revolves around the notion of children as 'real' readers who need 'real' books. It is a process in which school and home form a partnership with teacher and parent playing an equally important role. . .

So what's my problem? My problem is what happens when she starts school? As Liz Waterland says: schools should be good at teaching reading. The subject has had more pages of print devoted to it than any other aspect of primary education. The entire population of Britain should now be fluent readers, fully aware that books are life-enhancing and personality-developing, eager to read and to be caught up in the printed world. . .

Patently this is not so. Many people learn to read, more or less efficiently; very few become readers.

The crux of the problem seems to be reading schemes. I am aware – perhaps more so than the average parent – of the shortcomings of reading schemes: how it is the children who end up being labelled, levelled and colour-coded not the books; how a 'reader' becomes a special book not a person.

'Whatever is this book? Where did you get this?'

'It's a follow-up to one we read in class with Mr Merchant, funny and about school, a school like ours.'

'I don't care for the tone of it all. I don't like its language. Leave it. I'll get you a reader.'

Reader? But I'm the reader. Not the book.

from Gene Kemp, *Charlie Lewis Plays for Time*[5]

Looking at the school's reading

What are the right questions to ask about the school's existing practice assuming

– as we do! – that (a) you believe in a developmental view of learning and (b) you view reading as an active, interrogative activity?

1 Do the reading materials in use in the school communicate meaning?
This may seem an odd question. After all, what teacher would select books or a reading scheme which were meaningless? The uncomfortable fact remains, however, that some reading scheme materials can be 'read' from back to front without making any difference to the sense. I use the quotation marks advisedly! Print may have been translated into sounds by the inexperienced reader, but if no meaning has been communicated, can it really be said that reading has taken place? Furthermore, what is the effect on the young emerging reader when she or he encounters text without meaning? In an article called 'Reading Rickets and the Uses of Story', Barrie Wade draws attention to the 'potential conflict in the minds of children caused by any reading which promotes arbitrariness instead of pattern, disconnection rather than coherence and emptiness rather than fulfilment'.[6] Pattern, coherence and fulfilment are not bad qualities to keep in mind when considering the materials in use in classrooms.

2 Do the reading materials in the school contain a powerful sense of story?
Story is extremely important to us all: child or adult, experienced or inexperienced reader. Indeed Barbara Hardy has described story as 'a primary act of mind'. It is through story that we can come to terms with, and make sense of, the flow of experience that makes up our lives. To use Ted Hughes's phrase, stories are 'little factories of understanding'. As teachers we should read stories aloud to our children, not as time fillers but at high-status times of the day to signal their importance. We have a responsibility to provide books which contain a strong sense of story.

3 Are the materials interesting and enjoyable?
Our aim is to enable pupils to become autonomous readers who love books. We should look for books which are thought-provoking, which generate questions, and which will encourage the reader to talk about them with friends, family or the teacher. The text can be very simple; indeed, some pictures with little or no written text can generate great interest and enjoyment across a wide age range.

4 Do the reading materials relate closely to the language which children encounter and themselves use?
This really ties in with the sense of coherence and pattern mentioned earlier. The style of reading matter which is exemplified by 'can the rat pat the fat cat?' bears no relationship to the language in which the child is immersed at home, in the playground, in class – or anywhere else for that matter.

5 But do children have opportunities to learn about phonics and spelling patterns?
Much of this kind of work takes place when children are learning to write. It is clear that children do benefit from activities which encourage them to juggle and play with language through experiments with rhyme and rhythm in an assortment of word games. There is a world of difference between this kind of activity and

those which concentrate on children learning particular phonic rules out of context.

6 Do the materials acknowledge that the child lives in a society which is ethically, racially and culturally diverse?
'The Books for Students Guide to Children's Books for a Multicultural Society 0–7' suggests that teachers should look for:

- books which reflect a multicultural world in an accurate and balanced way. The majority of children's fiction publishing reflects a white world – our selection should seek to redress this imbalance and its implications of second-class status for ethnic minority groups. Non-fiction should be accurate and up to date, avoiding the association of 'white' with 'civilized', the presentation of all other cultures from a European (superior) point of view, and the depiction of all inhabitants of the Third World as poor, primitive, dependent on the west for aid and without history or culture.
- books in which people from all ethnic groups are shown in everyday activities and common experiences. Illustration and text should reflect naturally the multicultural nature of our towns and cities, showing adults and children from all ethnic groups shopping, going to school, playing, welcoming a new baby, feeling afraid, being happy.
- books in which children and adults from all ethnic groups in Britain are shown as positive people, taking responsibility, making decisions, being successful, respected and admired. These are much needed to counter stereotypes and encourage new attitudes; they are hard to find, especially with a contemporary British setting.
- books which make it possible to feel what it is like to belong to another ethnic or cultural group.

Fiction provides the most powerful route into empathy; non-fiction presented from the perspective of an individual from a different culture can provoke a strong imaginative response. Both can banish ignorance and pave the way to understanding.

Case study 2: reading at home

My niece is only 18 months old but already she has a clear idea of just how enjoyable stories can be. She now knows all about Spot and so dislikes coming to the end of a reading that she stops me from turning over the last page! She makes me go back to the beginning and start again. She hasn't even started talking yet. It seems to me that it is really important that schools tell parents just how vital it is to read books with very young children.

Case study 3: reading schemes

Glenys Kinnock does not mince her words when she talks about reading schemes – whether in private or public. Opening an exhibition recently at the National Book

League, she said that, without exception, such schemes were 'written in stilted and unnatural language'. She continued: 'With their zealous attention to controlled vocabulary and word counting, reading schemes give children no chance of ever understanding what they read, and it actually destroys the child's natural language. . .'

Glenys Kinnock speaks from personal experience. In the school where she now teaches, reading schemes have been entirely scrapped. Mrs Kinnock says that anyone who has taken the plunge will find the difference so great that they will never regret the step. She feels so strongly about the negative effects of reading schemes on children's performance and about how they reinforce a child's sense of failure that she even talks about there being a justification for 'burning books'.

But, she admits, teachers feel safer with a scheme. 'Teachers who are interested in the process of reading,' she says, 'will become more courageous. But it is all about hard-pressed teachers going into a whole new approach and that is quite frightening.'[7]

'I'm the reader, not the book'

So far this book has looked at some general issues about which the school needs to have a clear policy; now it will focus on the child – on what the 'reading journey' should feel like.

It helps to know what it feels like to be an insecure reader, to grapple with text that threatens never to make sense. Bob Moy's publication *Readers and Texts 1: The Reading Process*[8] suggests one way of reminding ourselves of failure (Figure 4.1).

Ereht saw llits on ngis fo eht srehto. Eht gnignis dah deppots sa yeht dehcaorppa eht pmac. Won ereht saw enoon ot eb nees. Neht yeht was no eht pot fo eno fo eth sexob a taerg etihw god.

Ti saw on derbhgueroht. Tub ti dah kcuts ot sti tsop – ekilnu eht rehto step. Yeht dah deraeppasid nehw eht elbuort tsrif nageb. Won yeht erew no eht tops. Yeht erew deppart.

Figure 4.1 A reading experience

For best effect, work with a partner. One of you should read the first paragraph. The other should read the second. Try to note carefully everything that happens to each of you each time: the effects on your body, your mind, your personality, your performance, your self-image, your general behaviour. For both of you, whether listener or reader, it is a salutary experience! We need to remember at all times the value of a supportive learning environment. Having said that, perhaps now is a particularly appropriate time to look at testing!

Testing

Although there is now a National Curriculum in place it is probable that the school will still use certain commercially produced reading tests. However, it is true to say that a number of tests commonly in use in schools have been around for a long time and therefore do not draw upon the most up-to-date research findings about the reading process. When looking at the school's reading test(s) – possibly with a view to making a change – a number of questions should be asked (and answered!):

1 Is the material which the child has to read in any kind of context, or is it in the form of isolated sentences or words? The more context there is, the likelier it is that the test will give useful data.
2 Is there any information which the test does not provide?
3 What are the results going to be used for? Is the test going to be used for screening children or for diagnostic purposes?
4 How long does the test take to administer? Here you may well have to weigh up the relative merits of a test which seems to fit your view of reading but which takes a long time to operate. Is there a compromise?

Progress in reading

The National Curriculum assessment procedures will offer some broad indications as to an individual child's progress through the Levels of Attainment, and complementary tests may well help you diagnose specific reading difficulties. However, it is important to remember that success in reading is, above all, rooted in enjoyment. In order to achieve Level 1 a child must 'show signs of a developing interest in reading' (1[c]); teachers can ask a number of questions about the reading activity of individual children which might throw more light on the nature of their growing interest.[9]

1 Does the child enjoy reading?
2 Is the child relating her or his own experience to what is read?
3 What kinds of texts does the child tackle with help?
4 What kinds of texts does the child tackle on her or his own?
5 Given twenty to thirty books, can the child choose one that she or he will enjoy or find informative?
6 Can the child do the same from a wider range, say fifty to 150 books?
7 How does the child cope with unfamiliar words? By semantic clues, syntactic clues, phonic clues or a combination?
8 What is the child's favourite book? Why?
9 Who is the child's favourite author?
10 What kinds of information does the child look for in books?

There are many different ways of recording children's reading behaviour including the widely used reading wheels designed by Liz Waterland and found useful by a large number of teachers.

Reading logs and diaries

A good way of discovering some answers to the questions above, while encouraging youngsters at the top end of the school to become more reflective in their reading, is to ask them to jot down their thoughts in a reading diary. It also moves the reader on from the rather limited 'book review' type of work!

Figure 4.2 provides an example which was devised for a class of 10 year olds, although it has been used successfully with other children too.

In using the diary idea it is worth bearing the following points in mind:

1 Don't use the diary laboriously. Nothing is worse than having to write in a log or diary every time a book is read. (Think how that would affect your own reading!)
2 There's probably no need to 'mark' it.
3 Try photocopying some pages for the rest of the class to read.
4 Writing about thoughts and feelings while they are reading, deepens understanding.
5 You might include some of the diary as part of a child's assessment portfolio.

The important thing to remember is that teachers have to become good at what Yetta Goodman calls 'kid-watching' if their assessments are to be interwoven with the learning process. The Primary Language Record, devised by teachers in London, offers a high quality but demanding support for teachers' observation of children's behaviour in reading and the other areas of language experience.

Looking at reading

An effective way of getting the staff to work together while looking at reading is to use readily available in-service materials such as the Open University's *Children, Language and Literature* pack.[10] This contains useful background source materials and a suggested outline for in-service work. These sessions can be adapted to suit your own needs and circumstances.

As a way into looking at reading development one school shortened the course into three 75-minute sessions:

1 Activities one, two and three which concentrate on teachers' own reading experiences.
2 Activities four and five (based on teachers surveying their pupils' reading experience).
3 A session based on 'Twenty-four things to do with a book' and celebrating a book which would form a core for a half-term's work.

They then returned and used more of the pack in ways they felt were right for them.

Figure 4.2   Reading diary

Title, author and cover	The ending
First impressions	
	I would/wouldn't recommend this book to a friend because . . . .
About halfway through	

It is important that you should have your own opinions about the books you read both in and out of school. The reading diary will help you in this. Try to write down your thoughts, feelings and ideas about what you read so that you make these clear to yourself, your teacher or other students in the class.

When you read a book use these notes to help you to write up your reading diary.

1 Title, author and cover
Note down what you think the book will be about, using any clues in the title, what you know about the author (if anything), the picture on the cover and any 'blurb'.

2 Your first impressions
Read the first dozen pages or so, stopping, if possible, at the end of a chapter or section.

Try to describe what you think and feel about:

(a) What has happened so far.
(b) The main characters in the book.

You might like to make a note of what you think is going to happen so that you can check later whether you are correct.

Write down any questions you want to ask.

3 Halfway through
Make a note of whether your thoughts or feelings about the story and the characters have changed. If they have, try to explain why and how. Think again about where the book is

Figure 4.2—continued

---

going. Make a note of your ideas about the way it will end or have changed. Explain why and make a note of what you now think will happen.

4 The ending
Look back over your earlier notes on this book.
   Write down your feelings about the way the book ended.
   Were you surprised?
   Say if you would recommend the book to people in your class and say why.

Words like 'good', 'bad', 'boring', 'all right', don't tell people reading your diary very much, so try not to use them in your diary.

The reading journey

Former HMI Trevor Dickinson has likened reading to a journey. I have found his list of statements a supportive introduction to school-based work on reading development. It is as follows:

- Reading grows out of talking, listening, experience – and reading.
- Literature encounters can benefit talking, listening and writing.
- Literature offers the possibility of pleasure.
- Reading success grows out of that pleasure.
- Reading to children offers the chance of strengthened relationships.
- Literature can powerfully feed the imagination.
- It can help generate independence of thought.
- It can help to increase understanding of ourselves and other peoples, places and times.
- It may enlarge sympathy.
- It can enlarge subject understanding across the curriculum.
- It is therefore important to teach children reading, rather than merely to read.
- Teaching reading is more a matter of example than method.
- Children's interpretation skills need developing.
- Promotion of voluntary reading improves standards.
- Poetry encounters are of special importance.
- The poet especially enables us to listen to language and to view the world afresh.
- School libraries need to be more powerfully used.
- We need to read to and with children more.
- We need to create the space and time for their quiet reading.
- We need to know more about what is available to read.
- We should look to the child's need for fantasy, myth and legend.
- We should hold to the best of both past and present.
- Children's reading life depends on our continuity and community of endeavour.

- We need to help chart their reading journeys.
- The nature of the reading start powerfully influences the reading future.
- Picture/story books are not only for the young.

You might try asking the staff to work in pairs and give them the following questions to get them started:

1 Which aspects of the reading journey does our school curriculum cover?
2 Is anything missing from Trevor Dickinson's agenda?
3 Do you disagree with any points?

You might then pick on one or two statements and, again in pairs, ask the staff to say what they think they mean. For example:

- What does 'Teaching reading is more a matter of example than method' mean in practice?
- What are the implications for the staff of needing to know more about what is available to be read?

Developing the book habit: a checklist

- book displays (chosen by pupils or teachers)
- reading places
- reading journals, diaries or logs
- book clubs
- class libraries
- school bookshops
- taped stories
- USSR (Uninterrupted Sustained Silent Reading)
- book weeks
- sharing sessions
- letters to writers
- readers from 'outside'
- paperbacks
- involve parents!
- telling stories
  etc.

Case study 4: involving parents

Dear

From Monday Feb. 11th, the children will be bringing home a plastic wallet with a reading book and a notebook in it. I usually put a comment in the notebook about how your child has enjoyed the picture book, what you can do to help him/her, and invite you to make a comment too, after you have shared the book with your child.

I would like to explain about the reading books themselves – as you will see, they are not books from reading schemes, not at all like the reading books that you, or perhaps your other children learned to read with. These books are called 'picture books', mainly because the pictures tell the stories and the words on the page are very simple and very obviously about the pictures on the page. This means that the children are given lots of clues about the words by looking at the pictures, and, because the book tells a short, interesting, simple story, the children will try to 'read' it. You and I will realize that they are not really 'reading' at this stage, but they are enjoying having a go! It is important that you give your child lots of praise and encouragement after his/her attempts. It is also important that you try and share the book with your child each evening – ten minutes each evening would be very helpful.

Please feel free to write in the notebook to me about how your 'reading at home' is going. Please send the folder into school every day.

I'm looking forward to working with you,

Best wishes.[11]

Chris Vallance, the teacher who wrote the letter above, argues convincingly about 'real' books. To conclude this section I would like to echo three remarks made by the same teacher:

A book is your friend for life.

If you have a spare five minutes, spend it with the parents not the child.

And, quoting from a parent's response:

We've listened to The Dark Dark Tale until it comes out of our Dark Dark ears!

Case study 5: a whole school response to a book

Chesworth Junior School was familiar with the integrated approach to learning by working within a theme, but when four of the teachers discovered *Railway Passage* by Charles Keeping (Oxford University Press), that approach took on a new meaning as a 'collective response' was developed. The teachers had classes of first-, second-, third- and fourth-year juniors; the enthusiasm of the teachers was apparent to their classes, and soon the contributions from the children supplemented and extended the initial ideas. The work was cross-curricular and there were so many excited reports buzzing between the four classes that integration extended beyond the curriculum and into the age-groups. Groups of mixed ability and age worked together productively and with an increasing independence of their teachers. *Railway Passage* had become a real place full of people and issues that mattered to the children. Characters' behaviour, circumstances and attitudes were criticized and analysed in lively discussion that then led to early draft procedures. Gradually, responses were modified, refined, perfected and finally given a public viewing in the form of a play, a puppet show and a gallery displaying art and craft work in a variety of media and a wide selection of rich and exciting language work. The results included in-depth studies of the central characters in the form of biographies and predictions; changes in the storyline; the creation of new characters; invitations to, role-playing and accounts of a street-party; an analysis

Figure 4.3 DARTS: directed activities related to texts

Deletion	Questions	Sequencing
(i) *Cloze* → Children discuss the most appropriate word to fit a gap left in the text, either a random gap or, say, every sixth word. The word(s) negotiated should make sense, be 'grammatical' and fit in terms of style. (ii) *Variations* → (a) Delete longer chunks (b) Compare versions with other groups and the original.	(i) **Open** rather than closed. Open questions (for example, why choose this title? what has the writer left out?) demand thought, provoke argument and alter traditional views as to the relationship between reader and text. (ii) **Pupils' questions** In pairs or threes, the children devise questions on the text (perhaps in role).	In small groups, the children are given a prose extract or poem cut into lines, segments or even individual words. By careful reading – and rereading – the group decides on an acceptable order. *This strategy works particularly well with verse.*

Prediction	Analysing text	Visual representations of text
The children, from their knowledge of a text, predict what is going to happen next. *This works well as a whole class activity with the teacher releasing text line by line, or section by section, using an OHP*	The children are asked to: underline [label] → or 'segment' text, for a specific purpose determined, probably, by the teacher. ('Segmenting': • isolating units of information • labelling of segments of text *without* teacher-provided labels.)	After reading the text, the children may draw maps, diagrams or complete tables – after due discussion!

All activities in small groups.

and criticism of structures and attitudes in society pertinent to the elderly people in the story; a 'film' of the book using the school's camera; poetry; stories and a range of art work that included cartoons, maps, diagrams, puppets, models, collages, portraits, drawings and paintings. The end product was rich and diverse, but the processes to achieve it had been so exciting and rewarding that they inspired interest among the rest of the staff who decided to participate in the next 'collective response'.

A search began for a new book, equally as inspiring as *Railway Passage* had been, that would allow a wide-ranging and flexible response to encompass the interests of about 360 children and their twelve teachers. *The Machine at the Heart of the World* by Jenny Wagner and Jeff Fisher (Kestrel Books) fulfilled all requirements and was appealing because the storyline was so open-ended. Again, after an initial staff meeting during which the end-date was chosen and integration of classes was planned, the project was introduced to the children who developed their own ideas which were duly included. This book encouraged an even wider curricular response with themes involving mathematics, computers, drama, art, design and technology, definitions of God and our place in the universe, environmental studies, the role of local government, music, science, the invention of problem-solving games and of course language development, all based on active discussion.

Once again, the end product of shows, performances, demonstrations and displays was rich and varied and reflected the motivation, application and enthusiasm of the children. Yet it was the more intangible responses, such as exhilaration and co-operation, that developed during the creative processes, which highlighted the feasibility of rich language development and its associated skills by using direct experiences. No textbook scheme of formalized exercises could generate such interest or inspire such a flow of living language.[12]

Case study 6: DARTS

I was concerned that some children in the school were not involved in the active comprehension of reading materials, particularly information books. I was also worried that some colleagues were reluctant to put aside comprehension exercises which were ineffective because they were not in a meaningful context.

The Head and I talked it over and agreed that we would make this issue the focus for a major INSET drive. We wanted to develop a range of strategies for active comprehension in the school. Some of us were already using cloze, group prediction and sequencing but we needed to broaden that repertoire.

I made good use of *Learning from the Written Word*, taking some interesting activities to use with the staff, asking them to attempt the tasks themselves, in small groups or pairs. I also made use of some fiction texts.

Figure 4.3 is an attempt to outline some of the DARTS activities. Some questions need to be considered:

- What size of groups?
- What kinds of text?
- What kind of talk occurs in the group?
- What strategies work best?

- When is a particular strategy appropriate?
- What are the benefits?

Arguably, DARTS work best:

- in smaller groups (of two or three).
- when the activity fits into a broader context, that is when the text isn't chosen at random.
- when the children understand that their response isn't 'right' or 'wrong'.
- when the texts fit the DART and both fit the group.
- when the strategy remains secondary to the text.[13]

Poetry

> At the moment, if you're reading poetry in a train, the carriage empties instantly.
> Andrew Motion[14]

> The teacher must love poetry but must not be a Poetry Lover, must never try to turn the thing into a sacred cow.
> Vernon Scannell[15]

One co-ordinator in a primary school was concerned that her colleagues appeared to be apprehensive about the teaching of poetry. She decided to set up a short introductory session with the staff. 'I was worried that not much poetry was being read and the poetry the children were writing was fairly ordinary.' The aim of the ninety-minute session was to introduce the staff to a range of resources which would help extend the language development work going on in their classrooms; draw on their own experience; give them a few ideas to try out; and get them writing themselves! The plan of the meeting looked like this:

1 I asked each member of the group to write down what they thought poetry was. After about five minutes we pooled the results.
2 We shared a 'why poetry' list and Ted Hughes's definition: 'Poetry . . . works with the imagination, perception and creative intuition; its tools are the essentials of all verbal communication used in its heightened and compressed way.'
   - It distils feeling
   - It is a charged treatment of language
   - It can be fun. The writer can experiment, even juggle with language
   - Words can be used:
     - as sound
     - as rhythm
     - as story
     - as pictures
   - A close contact with poetry:

- increases an awareness of how language works
- encourages precision in the use of language through compression
- increases an awareness of language through illusion and imagery
- it stimulates the imagination.

3 We read three or four poems which I had chosen as being as different as possible: rhymed, unrhymed, serious, comic and so on.

4 Then the tricky bit! I asked each member of staff to try writing a Dylan Thomas couplet, an Ezra Pound couplet, a form poem, syllable poem and haiku. (See examples from Brian Powell's *English through Poetry Writing*;[16] see 'Poetry Workshop' below.)

5 I warmly recommended Sandy Brownjohn's *What Rhymes with Secret?* and *Does It Have to Rhyme?*; the NATE-pack on Poetry and 'Thirty-Six Things to Do with a Poem' by Geoff Fox and Brian Merrick.[17]

6 We fixed a date for a follow-up meeting two weeks later when we were all to bring children's writing and discuss where we might go next. A poet in school maybe?

The meeting went very well, the staff enjoyed the writing, expressing genuine surprise at what they could do!

Poetry workshop

(a) Concise couplet-type devices based on the writing of Dylan Thomas. This employs hyphenated words, double-barrelled expressions, nouns used as adjectives and so on. You can start from:

Did you ever see a . . .?
e.g. Otter
silvery-sided, fish-fanged, fierce faced, mottled.

Examine why this is powerful. Try:
snake, poodle, cat.

Note:
'seeing' can be substituted by any of the senses.

(b) The capturing of a precise moment through the creation of a vivid image should also be encouraged through 'Ezra Pound couplets'. For example:

The apparition of these faces in the crowd
Petals on a wet black bough

A small tug pulling a mighty liner
An ant dragging a twig away

A full moon in a dark sky
A white plate on a blue-black table cloth.

The Form poem:

```
A  ── ── ── ──    4 words
B     ── ── ──     3 words
A  ── ── ── ──    4 words
B     ── ── ──     3 words
```

Every stanza has four lines. An ABAB rhyme scheme can also be used. For example: 'Steeplechase':

Sleepless, taut, sweating, tense.
Call-over, start, sprint.
Muddle, spreading, tiring, fence.
Trip, fall, splint.

Syllable poem:

```
                        Syllables
        ──                 1
      ── ──                2
     ── ── ──              3
    ── ── ── ──            4
  ── ── ── ── ──           5
    ── ── ── ──            4
     ── ── ──              3
      ── ──                2
        ──                 1
```

Haiku:

```
── ── ── ── ──        5 syllables
── ── ── ── ── ── ──  7 syllables
── ── ── ── ──        5 syllables
```

Haiku must be grammatically correct and use language economically and in a fresh way.

Figure 4.4 is an attempt to 'map' the possibilities for poetry work.

Library policy

School libraries work best when there is:

1 A policy for the Library and its development which relates to the aims of the school, discussed and agreed by the staff.

2 A short induction course for pupils on how to use the library.
3 Involvement of pupil librarians.
4
5
6

What others can you add? *Better School Libraries in Primary Schools* lists twenty![18]

Figure 4.4 'You have to inhabit poetry'

First encounters
Five-minute instant reactions: personal jottings.
A taped reading (by other children or teachers).
A poem a day (prepared, but *just* read).
TRAY computer program.
Display board.
Matching the poem to the current theme.

Sharing, presenting
Pairs or groups 'present' in *dramatic* form.
Pairs or groups prepare and *tape* their own versions of same poem.
Teacher-directed *choral* version.
Movement work.
Photograph to illustrate.
A frieze.
Map the story; devise a board-game, cartoon, mural.
A Poetry Week (pupil planned).
Focus on, say, pre-1900 poetry for half a term;
Poems from West Indies, USA, India, Africa, etc.
Collage.
Word-pictures: poem at the centre of a series of drawings.
Artwork and music.
Poems in Assembly.
WORD DANCE computer program.

Raising awareness and status
Accumulated personal anthologies.
Posters and artwork.
Learn a poem!
Taped anthologies.
Poets in schools.
Cassette collection.
Desert island poems.
Class anthologies.

Understanding, responding
Group discussions, with or without a guiding framework.
DARTS activities: cloze, sequencing, prediction.
Choose a title.

Figure 4.4—continued

Edit a poem.
Parody/imitation.
Illustrate a poem.
Invent a story behind the poem.
Retell the poem from another viewpoint.
Suppose I'd been her or him.
Rework the poem in another genre.
Alternative endings.
Play script.
Use alternative translations.
Extend the idea of the original poem.
'Doing' rather than analysing.
Just read it!
'That's how I see it';
'It makes sense like this';
Groups devise questions: factual or open-ended; to the teacher or other pupils.
Making Poetry:
    epitaphs
    haiku
    ballads
    shape poetry
    lyrics
    etc.

Finally

        Language develops where Roots and Reading cross.

                              Seamus Heaney

5 Media education[1]

> The school and the family share the responsibility of preparing the young person for living in a world of powerful images, words and sounds. Children and adults need to be literate in all three of those symbolic systems, and this will require some reassessment of educational priorities.
>
> UNESCO[2]

Until fairly recently, media education was widely regarded as being the province of secondary school English departments. However, it is becoming increasingly clear that the media have significant effects on the lives of children of all ages. The primary school needs, therefore, to have an explicit policy for media education. When we use the term 'media' we are referring to three areas:

1 Materials and technology:
   - pens
   - paper
   - film
   - newsprint
   - audio and video tape.
2 Institutions:
   - organizations
   - cinema
   - broadcasting companies
   - independent production groups.
3 Products:
   - printed materials
   - feature films
   - music tapes
   - television output.

Media education aims to make the connections between these areas explicit.

A study of the media should not be seen as yet another subject or curriculum area competing for space but rather as a context for language development work across the curriculum.

Working with a colleague, list the media products you use in your own teaching.

Although a wide range of media products are present in our classrooms, for the most part they are used uncritically. Videotapes, slides, schools programmes on radio and television are presented as objective statements of fact. The language co-ordinator should try to encourage her or his colleagues to develop critical approaches to the medium as well as the content.

Children need to develop skills to 'read' the images that they see on television, in advertisements, in comics, magazines and newspapers in a similar way to the way they are taught the skills of reading written text.

Teachers should also become aware that attitudes can be formed through a wide range of commercially produced materials which have less obvious, but none the less potent, messages. For example, one teacher I know has been doing interesting work with greetings cards and children's paintboxes where the colour pink is described as 'flesh-coloured'. Here media education and multicultural issues merge and need to be tackled together.

Fundamental to media education, then, is a belief that we should teach children that the media are involved in the construction of events and attitudes rather than in the clear-cut presentation of events as they happen. As Len Masterman puts it, 'communication forms are not "innocent" and transparent carriers of meaning. They are impregnated with values and actively shape the messages they communicate.'[3]

Many of the skills required to achieve these aims are familiar to teachers involved in active approaches to reading written texts:

- discussion
- sequencing
- analysis
- opinion
- deduction
- narration
- observation
- criticism
- prediction
- reading for a purpose
- recording
- comprehension
- hypothesizing
- negotiating
- decision-making.

You don't need a lot of expensive hardware, or a high level of expertise, to set up media education in your school. Interesting and valuable work can be based on the sorting out of order and meaning from pictures, cartoons, photographs or television sequences, storyboarding, designing an advertising campaign or simulating a newsroom.[4] Through this kind of practical critical activity children develop an understanding of how meanings are produced.

It is also valuable for pupils themselves to produce meanings through various media. Unless they experience research, planning, drafting, production and presentation, they are unlikely to appreciate the concept of mediation. In this way it is hoped that children can discover how material is selected and packaged to represent a version of reality.

A distinction should be drawn between production and the kind of practical activity suggested above. Production might, for example, involve the analysis and creation of a tape–slide presentation, a video or photo story.

As has been discussed earlier in the context of writing, a clearly defined sense of audience and purpose are critical. For example, is the tape–slide sequence for other children in the school, parents, old people and so on?

It is important to introduce the difficult area of media institutions. One strategy might be to talk about what goes on outside the frame of a picture, in order to examine what constraints, pressures and processes shape the final product.

Collect a number of photographs and pictures, maybe from colour supplements, and ask the following questions:

- Who made this photograph? This stimulates a consideration of human intervention, purpose and ownership.
- Where would you find this photograph? This question aims to highlight the importance of context, and how meanings are changed depending on where a text is seen.
- Who is it for? This focuses on the relationship between the creator/producer and the intended audience.
- How was it constructed? This question directs attention to the ways that members of a production team (e.g. lighting, props, make-up) contribute to the appearance of the product.

Finally

Cats' eyes glitter like diamonds but the cat is soft and furry as well, so the advert people are hoping people will say 'Oh look at that cat'. And the people are hoping that they will say, 'Oh look at that diamond necklace. Isn't it nice? I want it, please buy it.'

7-year-old commenting on a colour supplement advertisement

If there is one subject on which Kenneth Baker, the *Guardian*-reading parent and most teachers would actually agree, it is that children watch far too much television . . . I wouldn't even mind if they said, 'You mustn't watch TV while you're trying to do homework, you're not giving the television the proper attention it deserves'.

Katherine Whitehorn[5]

6 Drama for learning[1]

The function of the drama teacher is to challenge, arouse, interest, make anxious, give confidence, co-ordinate achievement, encourage reflection.

ILEA[2]

Drama works best when a teacher has the confidence and sensitivity to promote relationships with the children which are rooted in mutual respect and not in natural opposition. In such circumstances, drama can be used to extend and develop language, to make discoveries, to reach understanding and to explore the otherwise unreachable. It isn't 'acting', or even simply 'play', though it should retain the sense of fun that absorbs and stimulates; it shouldn't be teacher-dominated, but the teacher's role is central; it shouldn't be rigidly structured, but it needs shape and a clear sense of purpose. For some of us it can be disconcerting, since it appears to involve risk, but the real challenge lies in what it requires of the teacher in terms of establishing context and, subsequently, wise intervention:

> Left to themselves, with the teacher merely acting as facilitator by suggesting the context, providing an external stimulus, or commenting on an end product, the children are unlikely to create drama which extends them beyond what they already know.[3]

Not only is drama a strategy available to all primary teachers to use when they consider it appropriate but theatre also provides a means through which teachers and children can channel and share their work, adding new aspects to presentation. In short, drama provides an imaginative framework which, ironically, is 'safe' because it is not real. For all that, the 'suggestion of context' – the drama's starting point – is not something to leave to whimsical chance. As in all language-related activity, context matters; so too does planning.

Dorothy Heathcote refers on occasions to the importance of a 'press' being put on children's language: establishing a context and a motivation that, of itself, forces ideas, words and imagination. Clearly, then, decisions taken at the outset need to be firmly based on an awareness of the tension between the needs and experiences of the individual members of the class, and the overall shape of the on-going work.

There is a world of difference between someone in a class saying, 'Well, they should all take their belongings with them' and saying, 'Let's pack up and leave.' That is the switch I work for.[4]

It is an interesting professional dilemma, the balance between careful planning by the teacher using drama, and the freedom of the children to explore territory of their own defining and to establish a genuine contract between learners and teachers.

If the role play is to be successful it is also important that the teacher builds into this contract a clear sense of progression. This could well be organized under the following headings:

One:
- Select a specific aim for the lesson: what kind of learning do I wish to encourage through the drama? What do I want the children to learn about?

Two:
- Choose your context: which imaginative 'site' will the drama occupy? e.g. in the village, under sea, etc.
- Choose the children's roles. This does not mean casting! e.g. the class is divided into four groups each with a specific role.
- Choose your role and plan your possible point of intervention.
- Choose your 'frame' – the viewpoint of those in role. This includes a definition of the boundaries of the activity and takes account of control and safety issues.

Three:
- Devise activities for the children in role.
- Choose your focus: what is the imaginative purpose behind the activity? e.g. why are the divers under the sea?

Each of the following case studies is based on this flexible planning framework, the teacher, Kate Fleming, having worked with children in both KS1 and KS2 classrooms.

Case study 1: drama from story at KS1

The children (5–6 year olds) had been absorbed by the story 'Frederick' by Leo Lionnie, and it had promoted some lively discussion at a fairly high level.

The story is about a family of field mice preparing for hibernation, experiencing the cold winter days, and witnessing the solitary behaviour of Frederick. While the others gather and store food he gathers and stores his thoughts. The mice reproach him for his lack of industry, but he assures them that he is working, gathering and storing the rays of the sun, the colours of the countryside, and words for the long dark winter days when such things will also be in short supply. When the food runs out and the mice are cold and have nothing left to say to each other they turn to Frederick. He gets them to imagine the warmth of the sun, and recreates images of summer through the richness of his language.

Discussion with the children centred on the ways the seasons change, how to be an individual in a group, why we are all different each with something different to offer to society.

The opportunities for talking and writing needed to be exploited. I wanted to get away from simply acting out the story, believing that there was more potential in this context than this pretty routine approach usually offered.

I decided to start by getting the children to observe closely real mice and to note how they actually moved. We spent a long time on this, the children soon moving past their immediate response which involved a good deal of squeaking and rushing about. They explored with their noses, showing inquisitiveness by elongating and contracting their bodies; they travelled in short bursts; remained stationary, curled up; they climbed over each other rather than avoiding contact which gave their group movement a sense of fluidity.

With stage blocks we built the stone wall, the home of the mice in the story. The mice, apart from Frederick, were desperately trying to gather sufficient stores for the winter, so I introduced a range of actions related to work: gathering, lifting, pushing, dragging and storing. Using these words as starting points we developed a movement sequence linking in word patterns based on the mouse-like qualities we had considered previously. Discussion at this point concentrated on the urgency of animals preparing for winter.

The next session focused on what happened once the mice had hibernated. In the story initially everything was in abundance, especially words, and the mice entertained each other by telling stories suited to the occasion. They are described as stories 'of foolish foxes and silly cats' and we talked about what these might be about; what kind of things needed to be included; how they might have been told and the effect they might have had on the audience. The children then told each other stories and I stressed that the listener's response was as important as the telling. In the story winter continues, the stores are used up, the mice become cold and run out of things to talk about. Frederick then uses his own special supplies: colours and words. These he has stored during the plentiful times and now uses them to create imaginative situations so that the cold and hungry mice can forget their hardships.

We explored ideas about colours and the kinds of images that Frederick conjures up and I asked what the colours red, green, yellow and blue suggested to the children.

The story ends with Frederick's poem. I left those out of the original telling because I felt it was the weakest part of the book and also because I thought it would provide a focus for writing after the drama. I now felt that the children were sufficiently prepared for this writing activity and asked them to produce their own version of Frederick's poem, which they did in groups.

By the end of this activity the shape of the final presentation was becoming clear. This was organized into four interrelated units:

1 The mice in the wall movement sequence.
2 Work sequence with movement and word patterns.
3 Excerpts from the storytelling.
4 Poems performed by one or all of the group.

Case study 2: follow my leader – story from drama

The class of 7–8 year olds had only limited drama experience which had involved them in the occasional acting out of stories and some mime games. They had no experience of using drama as a way of refining and developing their thinking. Understandably they found working collaboratively difficult. My objectives were to use drama to help the children to create group stories and to provide contexts for a range of language activities including writing.

I introduced the game of 'Follow my leader', quickly splitting the line of children into five in order to have separate games. Once under way, with frequent changes of leadership, the game was played with varying degrees of complexity employing changes of pace and purpose (e.g. reluctance/enthusiasm or unsureness). We then discussed what the groups could do to make it look 'as if' they were following each other through different kinds of environments such as the back streets of a city, a desert, a jungle or even a totally alien environment.

Our discussion was focused by the two questions:

1 What can we do to make the environment look 'as if'?
2 What language ought we to use to make it sound 'as if'?

From this the class built up a drama vocabulary and started to develop movement, language and collaborative skills.

The children explored these ideas with growing conviction. I then introduced the idea that each group should encounter an environmental obstacle, discussing what the problem could be: possibly a river to cross, a mountain to climb, a ravine to travel through, or other dangerous territory to negotiate. The task now for each group was to choose a particular 'site' and to work out how the problem might be solved. It became clear that they could not do this until their narrative began to take shape. They needed to identify where they were, who they were and why they were there.

Soon there were:

a group of explorers mapping unknown territory in the rainforest;
a group of marines on a night manoeuvre in Scotland;
a group of botanists searching for a rare plant in the jungle;
a television crew making a wildlife programme in a remote part of Borneo;
a group of astronauts on an unknown planet.

The children worked through the drama, and started to develop various narratives which were refined further by a second sequence of questions:

● What was their expertise?
● Where did their special responsibility lie?
● What kind of complications could develop; what could the outcome be?

The children now had time to try out the drama, making sure that each member of the group felt comfortable with their role in the story and that all the ideas had been fully aired. They knew that they were going to share their stories, but I doubted the value of five separate performances knowing that the children did not possess an adequate range of theatrical skills to undertake such a task.

I then asked the children to focus on a specific event in their story and to prepare a single frame in the 'film' of their story on one of the following areas:

- The most exciting moment
- The most frightening moment
- The moment of rescue
- The moment of despair
- The moment of realization.

We discussed each frame using the following questions as starting points:

- How do you think the medical officer feels?
- What happens next?
- What were the events leading up to this situation?
- What is the dialogue?

Placed in roles as photographers the rest of the class decided on the best angle for each group tableau and we 'took photographs' of each dramatic moment.

Each child then had a well defined context for recording their stories and they chose the form most appropriate for their particular role. Some children chose to use audio tape while others chose to do their writing on the wordprocessor. The writing adopted a wide range of different forms and included: official logs, letters targeted at different audiences, medical reports, newspaper articles, diary entries and reports on tape for radio and television programmes.

All the writing was accompanied by appropriate photographs, drawings, maps or plans. The children wanted their work to look authentic and took considerable trouble to make it as real as possible.

Case study 3: building a community – creating a context

The children, from Y6, were experienced in drama and generally able. I wanted to create a context, in this case a village community, through which we could explore issues of gender and class while providing opportunities for speaking and listening and writing.

The project was organized into three sessions although discussion and writing were also carried out in other areas of the curriculum.

The children worked enthusiastically on large pieces of paper on the hall floor while brainstorming their ideas about villages. These were pooled, discussion centring on the credibility of thatched cottages, duck ponds, village shops and vegetable gardens. Interestingly, the children thought that this view was over-romanticized, but they did have some pertinent things to say about nostalgia. As they gathered round to look at a map of an imaginery village they soon began to interpret what they saw: forest, river, cricket pitch and the central focus of the stately home.

In small groups they were asked to select a point on the map and tell the rest of the class what they could see from this point. I placed emphasis on accurate description and encouraged the class to employ all of their senses while considering the atmosphere created by the time of day, season and weather.

The second session began with a now familiar map and discussion which focused on the age of the village. The children discussed what evidence there was that this was an old settlement. Back in their groups the children were then asked to choose an imaginary event that may have happened in the village. At this point the children created a tableau representing the most significant moment within their historical event. This was presented in the form of a still photograph and caption for the village museum.

The third session began with the map again. This time the discussion focused on:

- What kind of village it was
- What sort of people live there now
- If the children lived there, who would they like to be?

The children now decided which role they would like to take on. They considered questions of age, type of job, family structure, where they lived, neighbours and what kind of personality they possessed.

At this stage I did not worry if two children had chosen the same house or occupation knowing that this would sort itself out in due course.

The next activity started with a still photograph based on life in the village. I asked the children to group themselves with people they would be likely to mix with and to think of an activity. I gave them five settings: the village pub, the post office, the stately home, the school and the garage. Three children opted to stay on their own, one was an old lady who was housebound, one was a writer who was a recluse and one because he was a farmer who needed to be at work. Within these settings the children had to devise an incident which they shared in tableau form: they then improvised a resolution to the incident.

Individually I asked the children to imagine it was evening and also that they were writing their diaries on the happenings of the day. In turn, each child then read out their entry for that day.

I now felt that the children's belief in the village was sufficiently strong to introduce the problem which I hoped would focus their learning. The map now had an added feature: across the stately home was stuck a large 'SOLD' notice. I had also put up posters which advertised a village meeting to discuss the sale and which let the villagers know that the property developer who had bought the estate would be at the meeting to answer any questions.

The children had to decide how they felt about the sale and I encouraged them to get into groups to work out the kinds of questions they were going to ask at the public meeting. I was in role and chaired this meeting having created a character in a previous session, a colleague, also in role, had agreed to attend the meeting as the property developer. The meeting turned out to be highly vocal, all of the children had a point of view and all were keen to ask questions. A wide range of issues were discussed and the meeting closed with the intention that the village would fight the planning permission. In turn, this led to a variety of writing activities and research.

A policy for drama

Drama makes it possible for both teachers and pupils to escape from the more familiar patterns of language interaction which exist in the classroom and offers them both a new range of possibilities.

O'Neill and Lambert[5]

Drama's contribution to the language work in a school can be extensive and far-reaching: Figure 6.1 is a checklist aimed at helping you to evaluate the school's policy for drama.

> Without a co-ordinated policy in drama in the school, the amount of drama done depends largely on the enthusiasm of individual teachers . . . Yet the potential for Drama here is enormous. This emphasis on developing children's play and learning through discovery can lead into, and be greatly developed by, a progression into more structured drama experiences.[6]

Do the staff:		*Where do we focus our attention?*
1 (i) make use of professional theatre-in-education?	(ii) prepare adequately for it and then follow it up?	
2 (i) understand the difference between 'drama' and 'theatre'?	(ii) practise drama skills 'within a chosen context and as an integral part of the dramatic process'?[7]	
3 (i) have an appropriate space available?	(ii) and appropriate time?	
4 (i) value continuity?	(ii) plan for continuity?	
5 (i) evaluate work in drama?	(ii) involve the children in evaluation?	
6 value the 'learning contract in drama'?[8]		
7 make drama a regular feature of work?		
8 *all* get involved?		

Figure 6.1   What should a policy for drama incorporate?

Finally

> Reflection is the only thing that makes Drama worth doing. If you cannot increase reflective power in people, you might as well not teach, because reflection is the only thing in the long run that changes anybody.
>
> Dorothy Heathcote[9]

7 Micros and language work

The microcomputer can be a word processor, a bank of information upon which to draw, a storehouse, a moving page of text or pictures, a focus for discussion. It can produce newspapers, ask and answer questions, check your spelling, give you the facility to play with language. It still holds a fascination for most of us which can be both stimulating and daunting in the classroom, perhaps both at the same time!

For writers, reluctant or otherwise, it radically alters the rules of the game: you can juggle, manipulate, delete and play with words. At the push of a button, children can get a convincingly 'real' product. It brings home to them the value of drafting and editing.

For readers, the micro can allow you to sidle up on the text: programs like TRAY are a flexible and stimulating means by which pupils can explore a poem, or a piece of text, almost without noticing how they are being drawn in.

We are working now in a world where children accept the power of the computer as readily as they do television or radio. Classrooms which are communities of real writers and real readers should not deny children access to that power.

Figure 7.1 is a summary of the range of possibilities the micro offers language work.[1] That this chapter isn't any longer is a reflection of my belief that the micro should permeate all aspects of language work; I do not see it as a separate issue.

Figure 7.1 The microcomputer's contribution to language work

Function	Contribution	Program	Comment
1 Word processing	Redrafting. Automatic Tippex. It allows the movement of whole paragraphs: insertion/deletion of individual words or whole sentences. 'Real' product.	EDWORD VIEW WORDWISE PLUS BEELINE QUINKEY PROMPT/WRITER PHASES 2 PENDOWN FLEXIWRITE	'I have seen a child move from a total rejection of writing to an intense involvement . . . within a few weeks of beginning to write with a computer.'[2]
2 Simulation and adventure games	A framework for purposeful talk. Incorporates decision-making, problem-solving; can include role play, code-breaking, language activities. The micro here offers speed of response, graphics and sound.	L MALLORY MANOR GRANNY'S GARDEN ADVENTURES DRAGON WORLD SPACE MISSION MADA FLEET ST PHANTOM TELETYPE	'We should avoid programs that merely divert.'
3 Information handling	Pupils can devise their own data files for *real* purposes. An important area for developing the skills of interrogating a data-base, finding things out: 'Asking questions, getting answers.'	INFORM GRASS DATASHOW OUR FACTS KEYNOTE MAGPIE	

4 Newspapers, etc.	Programs which provide for newspaper production, news handling and teletext.	FRONT PAGE FLEET STREET EDITOR EXTRA ⟶ MICROFAX ⟶ FRONT PAGE EXTRA ADVANCED FOLIO NEWSPAPER NEWS BULLETIN DESKTOP STORIES	For newspapers. Simulates news inflow. Simulates Teletext.
5 Word play and language	Programs which invite exploration of text. Pupils can experiment with words, shape, colour and movement in writing poetry.	IMAGE TRAY ADD-VERSE WORD-DANCE POD INTRO TRAY MUDDLES PODD	Avoid electronic 'language exercises'
6 Electronic mail	Allows a text message to be sent to another 'mail-box'. It will arrive in seconds and can be read whenever the recipient wishes.	THE TIMES NETWORK SYSTEMS CAMPUS 2000 CHEAP FAX MACHINES	

'Like language, the computer reaches across the curriculum: that similarity is significant and potentially powerful.'

'Computers offer marvellous opportunities in language, still largely unexplored, but they must be used intelligently. Teachers, not computers, must be in charge of what goes on in the name of language education, which means that teachers must understand computers and not be afraid of them.'[3]

8 Knowledge about language

It is not learning about language that makes you a better user, but it is becoming a better user that makes you interested in language.

Pam Czerniewska, Director, National Writing Project

It is necessary, rather, to recognise that we need both accurate descriptions of language that are related to situation, purpose and mode (i.e. whether the language is spoken or written), and prescriptions that take account of context, appropriateness and the expression of meaning.

English for Ages 5 to 16: 4.20

The publication of The Kingman Report in the spring of 1988 came at the end of a year's deliberation by the Government Committee of Inquiry set up to advise on the teaching of English Language. Its terms of reference were far more restricting than those of the Bullock Committee a decade or so earlier. For example, it was asked to state 'what, in general terms, pupils need to know about how the English Language works and in consequence what they should have been taught, and be expected to understand, on the workings of the English Language, at 7, 11 and 16'. The Cox Committee drew upon the findings of Kingman in the knowledge that what it recommended was likely to become enshrined in National Curriculum Orders. The members of the Kingman Committee had not been similarly constrained. However, in making a case for a wider knowledge about language (now widely abbreviated to KAL) by all pupils, Cox reiterates many of the points stressed in the *Primary Language Book* and also states that: 'knowledge about language should be an integral part of work in English, not a separate body of knowledge to be added on to the traditional English curriculum'.[1]

Following on from the Kingman and Cox Committees' work the DES funded the Language in the National Curriculum Project (LINC) which ran from April 1989 to March 1992. The main aim of the LINC Project was to develop the model of language outlined in the Kingman Report. However, this model was not placed in the context of teaching and learning. It was the intention of the LINC Project to remain true to the spirit of Kingman but make it 'pedagogically sensitive'.

Kingman, Cox and the LINC Project all emphasize:

1   That old-fashioned grammar teaching is not appropriate.
2   That language is powerful.
3   That language changes over centuries and between generations.
4   That literature is an important part of pupils' entitlement.
5   That drafting is an important part of the writing process.
6   That wordprocessors help the writing process and encourage pupils to reflect upon language.
7   That context, audience and purpose are central to language development.
8   That media studies should be one of the language experiences youngsters enjoy.
9   That talk is different from writing, but as important and that the differences should be made explicit.
10   That children should be encouraged to reflect upon their own performance.
11   That language – and an interest in language – is developed through use not analysis.
12   That teachers and pupils need a shared language for talking about language, that is, a meta-language.

One very important question which remains unanswered by any of the reports, the LINC Project, or by research, concerns the relationship between pupils' knowledge about language and their ability to use language effectively. The connection seems plausible but is not proven. Indeed, the Kingman Report was slightly misleading in that it simplified the subtle process whereby a sensitive and knowledgeable teacher intervenes at the critical time in order to help the pupil reflect meaningfully on the language being used. It is not simply a matter of 'knowing' technical names for bits of language, but rather of understanding 'that communication depends both upon an awareness of circumstances, and on the processes and means by which writing or speech can be shaped in order to mean something'. There is a crucial difference between knowing *that* and knowing *how to*.

We would not wish to shift from the view of language typified by the remark of Pam Czerniewska at the outset of this chapter, or indeed from Edward Blishen's words below. At the same time, it seems appropriate to suggest reflection and discussion about the kind of language curriculum that underpins this book and is at its most apparent in Chapters 2, 3 and 4. In doing so, I would suggest that your colleagues and yourself consider questions stimulated by the Kingman and Cox Reports.

● What is it in a pupil's progress that determines when implicit knowledge about language should be made explicit?
● What do the children in your class already know about language?
● What can children in your class say about the language of their own community?

- What knowledge about language do you need to know in order to improve an individual child's performance?
- How should pupils develop:
  - an ear for language?
  - tolerance of other languages?
  - an interest in language as a phenomenon?

The final word

I remembered old Judy . . . who turned language into a sort of verbal Meccano. It was all spanners and nuts and screws. I loved language and was deeply curious about its operations, but shrank from being asked to think of it as a branch of mechanics. . . As a professional writer . . . I simply think that most of us learn to use language by using it: far less by analysis than by synthesis, its marvellously serviceable twin.

Edward Blishen

9 Liaison for continuity, or Les Liaisons Dangereuses

The cast

Fred Thompson	Head of English, Sir Peter Lorre Comprehensive
Val Hewitt	Deputy Head and Language Co-ordinator, St Peter's C. of E. Junior
George Fox	Head of the Pines County Primary School
Janice Woods	Language Co-ordinator, Milton Park Primary
Doreen Sansom	Friend and colleague of the Language Co-ordinator, Park Vale Primary
Trish Blackwell	Language Co-ordinator, Bicknell Lane Primary
Jane Anderson	Teacher-in-charge, Lower School English, Sir Peter Lorre Comprehensive

The scene

The staffroom of a sizeable comprehensive at 4.30 in the afternoon. A group of chairs has been pulled together in a corner and an electric kettle is steaming on a ledge nearby. One or two teachers drift through to flick at notices on the bulletin board, to rummage in their pigeon-holes or to swap pleasantries about decorating, squash, car service costs or Wayne Phipps in 3X. Fred Thompson is scattering a packet of Rich Tea biscuits on to a plate; Val Hewitt is seated and occasionally glances at her watch. The other visitors arrive one by one and sit down.

Fred: Anyone for coffee? Only instant I'm afraid . . . and it's powdered milk. Kettle's boiled. [*Val Hewitt looks at her watch again. There is a pause as some people take coffee.*] OK. Good to see you again. It doesn't seem a year ago since we all met to chat about liaison.

George: Sorry to interrupt but Ted Grainger, Tony Brown, Hilary Freeman, and Veronica Wilson send their apologies.

Doreen: So does Jane Jackson. She asked me to come in her place, if that's OK. I've got responsibility for Maths.

Fred: OK, thanks. Well time's pressing on so I'd better let you know what's happening in the first and second year. In fact, Jane, could you fill in our guests since this is really your area?

Jane: [*surprised*] Yes . . . er . . . fine . . . Well, as you probably know we don't set in year one but leave the kids in their tutor groups. We aim to get them to read at least two books a term and we give them a crash course on the basic skills – you know, the apostrophe, speech marks, that sort of thing. One problem is that quite a few kids have already read some of the books and it's pretty boring for them. Fred and I have discussed this and wonder if we can't come to some sort of arrangement about titles.

Fred: [*surprised*] Oh . . . yes . . .

George: I recognize that you're the English experts and the department does a good job, but why the crash course? I'm sure I speak for my colleagues when I say that we all give a lot of attention to this area.

Fred: Yes of course, it's just we like to reinforce the excellent work going in our feeder schools.

Val: Can you tell me how you use the yellow record cards that we fill in each year?

Fred: Sorry? Yellow cards? Jane, do you get to see them?

Jane: They usually go to the year tutor, although, of course, we can have a look if we need to!

Trish: Going back to the point about agreeing over titles, we might find that difficult because we run a book box system with a fairly wide range of individual readers.

Janice: So do we. Some of the kids will have read all of your titles. One of mine is into Dostoevsky. [*Fred and Jane glance at each other.*]

Fred: Anyone for another coffee?

Val: I'm sorry I've got to make tracks. I'm picking up Trevor from swimming.

Fred: Thanks . . . er . . . Val.

The meeting drifts on for another half hour or so and then breaks up with a resolution that they must all get together more often.

Of course, we recognize that this is an exaggeration, a caricature, but is there anything to learn from this extract?

Some questions

1 Who do you think has called this meeting?
2 How do you think the primary teachers view their secondary colleagues?
3 How do you think Fred and Jane view their primary colleagues?
4 Is there a way of solving the difficulty over books?

5 Can you detect any other factors which might prevent the group operating successfully?

Creasey, Findlay and Walsh (1983) point out that liaison is the human face of the process whereby we attempt to achieve a continuum of experience for each youngster across the primary/secondary transition.[1] They identify a number of factors which work against the establishment of continuity through liaison.

1 Specialist teachers representing secondary schools vs generalist teachers of the primary schools.
2 This leads to misunderstandings and difficulties of communication if liaison meetings are instigated.
3 A wide range of different approaches to learning within the feeder primary schools.
4 Misunderstandings over the audience, the purposes and uses of records and other transfer documents.

● Can you identify any other constraints?

Some principles

1 Initially try to meet on neutral ground – a teachers' centre or professional centre. This helps to avoid the 'we're coming to tell them how to do it syndrome'.
2 Try not to set up meetings which are just 'to talk about' liaison; they rarely achieve much. Get people doing things.
3 Plan a series of meetings, not just a one-off to satisfy the demands of a head or a policy statement.
4 Try to identify an area of common concern and work together on it. If both primary and secondary colleagues develop common approaches and styles, then continuity is more likely to be achieved. Maybe 'commission' an adviser to help run a short course to get it going.
5 Alternate or rotate the chair of the meetings so as to avoid a feeling of either secondary or primary dominance.
6 If possible, exchange teachers or set up class to class, pupil to pupil links across the phases.
7 Establish a common view of record keeping; nothing is worse than to spend a long time filling in details which you know are unlikely to be used.
8 Often a good starting point is for each member of the group to bring along one or two pieces of work which they would like to share with colleagues.
9 Remember that it's difficult to achieve continuity between schools if there is no sense of real continuity existing within schools – class to class or year to year.
10 Joint publication of an anthology of writing from, say, the final year of primary

and the first year of secondary is often a worthwhile enterprise since it involves purposeful debate about writing among the teachers involved.

11 There are interesting possibilities in devising a programme of work that crosses the transition, in other words, the pupils take an on-going project through to the first term of secondary. The planning of such a scheme has obvious benefits.

Finally

'Miss Beale said you would show me round, to look at the projects', said Andrew.

'Why, do you want to copy one?' asked Victor . . . 'You could copy mine, only someone might recognize it. I've done that three times already.'

'Whatever for?' said Andrew. 'Don't you get tired of it?'

Victor shook his head and his hair. 'That's only once a year. I did that two times at the junior school and now I'm doing that again', he said. 'I do fish every time. Fish are easy. They are all the same shape.'

'No they're not', said Andrew.

'They are when I do them', said Victor.

From Jan Mark, *Thunder and Lightnings*[2]

10 The role of the head

A manager has to cut his coat according to his cloth – he has to mould his team's style to the players available. The same applies to the individual player. None of them is perfect, so you have to develop their strengths and cover or reduce their weaknesses. It is up to the manager to study players, to recognise certain factors in their playing ability as well as their characters and make up.

Bob Paisley, ex-manager, Liverpool FC[1]

Case study 1: the benevolent dictator

Management style? I suppose it depends on your language co-ordinator. In my case, I inherited a set-up and a language post-holder to go with it. Pretty soon after I arrived, we held an open staff meeting to look at the curriculum documents that existed in the school. We all agreed that any policy documents we had should reflect the people who were doing the teaching. Staff change meant policy change, I suppose.

I was keen to focus on language and maths and the rest of the staff agreed! It's how you phrase things – you get 'em to think *they* thought of it. We had a staff of eight then – it's six and a half now and everybody was involved somehow or other in the next phase. The language co-ordinator and two other members of the staff looked at the 'old' language documents and reported back six weeks later. The papers had a mid-1970s feel about them, they didn't actually say anything. Bare statements, nothing more – 'We do reading', that sort of thing. No one on the staff felt they had any ownership of what was written, and our ideas had changed too. Especially on reading, mainly because of local in-service courses and the OU Language and Reading courses.

We hammered out some draft proposals. We argued, mostly about reading, though there was some disagreement about handwriting too. The debate over reading was interesting: several of the staff were well into Cliff Moon approaches. You know, personalized reading, real books. But there were a lot of parental pressures that were pulling us the other way. I admit I did wonder if the language co-ordinator had gone overboard. Throwing the baby out with the bath water. I suppose this is where the head comes in – evaluating what's going on, having an overall view. You've got to be capable of defending what you're doing by being able to quote chapter and verse. The buck stops with me. . . .

I was more personally involved I reckon with the handwriting issue. I didn't want to be dictatorial, but I was taught italic script at primary school and found I couldn't write when I got to secondary school. Terrific! Anyway I kept out of the way and left it to the deputy. It took longer maybe, but it was better that I kept out of that one.

Then the teachers' action started and everything started to go wrong. It was very frustrating for all of us. There were some lunchtimes when I just sat alone in the staffroom, just me and the infant-helper. Nobody else.

Where are we now? It all depends crucially on the staff, though the reading issue has to be resolved by me. It's as if the staff lit the fuse and then felt they couldn't go back. We spent a lot of money on 'Kaleidoscope' for instance, and there are some clear benefits, but we cannot have a policy which permeates one part of the school, but which dies the death higher up.

We see all this as on-going. What we have in writing should be updated through open discussion. I've been conscious of the value of raising the language co-ordinator's status in the school. It's a consequence of standing back (most of the time!) and letting her determine the direction. I believe in making sure she knows she's doing a good job – when she is! It's also necessary to question and criticize when it's appropriate. If it's bad, you say it's bad, reasonably nicely!

I'm lucky the co-ordinator is good – all that on MPG! – and she's a team leader as well. That certainly makes life difficult for her. I make sure that I find time for her, for example, by teaching her class sometimes.

The fact that we work in an open-plan school makes it much easier to monitor what's going on. I can listen in, talk to the kids. You can be observing, but merely doing a bit of computing. You'd have to be a moron not to know what's going on. You're part of the team. I sit in the staffroom with them most of the time – they need some escape to moan about me!

I'm more benevolent than dictatorial, though it might be different in a different school.

Case study 2: the patient head[2]

At the moment the problem is that I've inherited a language post-holder who finds it all pretty tough going. It's not that she's unwilling to go on courses – I've encouraged her to do that – but that she comes back with a series of 'one-off' ideas which never seem to fit together or have any coherence.

I think that the language job is probably the most taxing in the school. You're not just dealing with such areas as the reading policy or spelling or poetry, but the way pupils learn. This means you're also concerned with the way your colleagues run their classrooms. All this on MPG, or maybe in a bigger school, MPG + A.

The ideal language co-ordinator has to be a first-rate classroom practitioner: someone who can lead by example, really show how a good idea can be put into practice. At the same time, she must be tactful and supportive even with what we might call 'hesitant' colleagues. If the co-ordinator is threatening, people are turned off. She must be well informed and be able to explain why (as well as showing how) existing practice should be developed, adjusted or abandoned. I think a clear theoretical foundation is important but not one encrusted with masses of jargon; that really puts people off!

Anyone involved in curriculum development has to be patient, even heads. Things don't happen overnight. If I had an effective post-holder, she would probably work on one area for two years with two or maybe three teachers drawing in other people when appropriate. The head and the governors determine overall school policy but in consultation with those teachers carrying posts of responsibility. Because language and learning are interlinked, the good language co-ordinator has a vital role to play in conjunction with the head.

Case study 3: 'too important to give it away!'

An adviser came in not so long ago and, after the preliminary chat about this and that, asked me who my curriculum post-holders were and how they were getting on. Everything went well until I revealed the awful truth that I didn't actually have a language co-ordinator. At first this didn't seem to go down too well but I explained that I thought that it was such an important job that the head should do it herself.

I've worked in schools where a language co-ordinator had real problems when she tried to get other teachers to take on new ideas. It was fine as long as the co-ordinator just ordered new bits of the reading scheme, or rewrote parts of the syllabus or policy document, but as soon as she attempted to get real changes of approach in the classroom, she came up against a brick wall.

The job of the language co-ordinator is really quite different from that of any other curriculum leader; it should really be called the learning co-ordinator because that's what it's about. It's not about spelling policies or deciding to use this reading scheme or that, but about how effectively the children learn across the curriculum. Language is the medium for learning in all areas.

In order to get teachers to change what they do in the classroom – how they organize learning to allow all kids to use their own language – you have to have status. Unless they are exceptional, I don't think that an MPG teacher has the necessary status. The head is the person who has ultimate responsibility for the curriculum so the head should take on the role of language co-ordinator.

Of course this doesn't mean a dictatorial approach – far from it. I consult with my teachers over language issues as often as possible and we negotiate courses of action. But, ultimately, it's my responsibility to see that things happen – and that certain things stop happening!

From the three case studies, what do you see as being the characteristics of:

- a good language co-ordinator?
- a good head?
- a good working relationship between the head and language co-ordinator?

11 Managing change: the language co-ordinator's support pack[1]

Organizations are dynamically conservative: that is to say, they fight like mad to remain the same. Only when an organization cannot repel, ignore, contain or transform the threat, it responds to it. But the characteristic is that of least change: nominal or token change.

Donald Schön, 1971 Reith Lecture

We trained hard, but it seemed that every time we were beginning to form up into teams, we would be reorganized. I was to learn later in life that we tend to meet any new situation by reorganization, and a wonderful method it can be for creating the illusion of progress while producing confusion, inefficiency, and demoralization.

Caius Petronius, AD 66

There are two central questions which a language co-ordinator must ask:

1 Which are the areas of priority needing attention in the school?
2 Which teachers will it be most productive to work with?

In Chapter 1 we have already looked at the question of priorities. The following activity takes that issue further as well as addressing the second question. There are no right or wrong answers. You may find it useful to work with a friend, colleague or your headmaster on what follows.

Holmbury Down School

Holmbury Down School has 210 pupils aged between 5 and 11. They come from a privately owned housing estate whose parents are very supportive of the school. There is within the catchment area a small council estate, and the children from these houses are seen by some staff to be the cause of the problems in the school. The building was erected in 1958 and adapted to 'open plan' in 1975.

There are seven teachers and a very newly appointed headteacher, Mr Brownspear, who wishes to change the ethos of the school. The previous head had been in control for twenty-three years. Mr Brownspear causes some concern among the parents: he arrives on his bicycle each morning and he usually wears crew-necked sweaters. The only time he has worn a suit was for his interview. He jogs every lunchtime and, consequently, getting to talk to him is difficult!

One of the reforms he is keen to institute concerns the school uniform. At present the children wear blue pullovers and grey trousers or pleated skirts: Mr Brownspear is now negotiating with a London firm to supply sweatshirts (with an individual logo) and coloured jeans to replace the existing uniform.

The deputy head, Miss Graham, runs the school, and everyone is aware of this (in fact, many parents believe she should have got the headship). Her classroom is a very 'tight ship'. Every child's desk is a perfect model of tidiness and her stock-room is a joy to behold, partly because its contents tend to remain on the shelves. The children love being in her class. The always know precisely what is expected of them and the work follows a regular annual pattern of activities. Miss Graham has been at Holmbury Down for twenty-four years and she knows the exact details of almost every child and indeed has taught a significant number of the children's parents. She was originally appointed to the school as PE teacher, but now she 'looks after' the ordering of all materials. She does not agree with many of the changes that Mr Brownspear is trying to effect but would never let any member of staff know this. She has, however, expressed her worries over it to her mother with whom she lives.

The other seven teachers include two women nearing the ends of their careers. Both married, they teach very much in the way that they have always done, although they do, now and again, try some new approaches that are put in their way. Then there is a rather younger woman, who since she is a vegetarian, cannot supervise school meals: the sight of meat she finds offensive. She was redeployed from a nearby secondary school. On MPG, she does not wish to be considered for promotion, not least because she leaves school very early three times a week to work out at 'Shape Health Studio'.

Mr Grant is on MPG + A with responsibility for PE and history: the children are just a little afraid of him as he is very large and tends to become rather irate if the school loses netball or football matches against Holmbury Edgehill, which is the nearest primary school to the 'Down'. Although Mr Grant teaches in a very formal and traditional manner, he often talks in the staffroom about his interest in an integrated curriculum, before remarking that he has not yet had time to put it into practice; he has however done some quite masterful basketry with the more able children.

Music is taught throughout the school by Neville Green, aged 25. Neville has some problems with class control, particularly with the top three classes. The children often comment on his purple trousers, but he was responsible for quite an unusual Early English Chorale at Christmas which elicited a lot of comment.

Ms Annette Laporte is the part-time teacher of French, married to the local restaurant owner.

Very recently Mr Brownspear appointed Caroline Laycock to be on MPG + A with responsibility for language development throughout the school. She is young, earnest and committed. She has offered (possibly a little too quickly) one or two new approaches which have had a mixed reception from the rest of the staff. Caroline discovered that the reading scheme is 'Janet and John' until the second year, after which there is a free choice of reading. The main English texts are by Ronald Ridout, and these are very widely used in all classes. Most of the books are very old, but they have been carefully repaired with Sellotape by the secretary. (There are supposed to be a large number of new books in a cupboard near to Mr Brownspear's office, but he has lost the key and no one has yet managed to open the door.)

Holmbury Down has a very active PTA. The chairman is Harry Ross, a local coach operator. He recently bought a new set of football shirts for the school team bearing the legend 'All the way with "The Down" and Harry Ross'.

Caroline wants to make changes and has secured the support of her head.

- List the difficulties you feel she might encounter at Holmbury Down. Are there any solutions?
- Look at the list of possible areas of interest in Chapter 1 (on page 3). Are there any missing?
- Work out which three areas you would recommend to Caroline to try first at Holmbury Down
- Who should Caroline try to work with?
- Compare your own school to Holmbury Down and attempt the same activity!

Although the majority of language co-ordinators who have taken part in activities like the one described above concede that they must continue to develop their own knowledge and expertise in this area, the starting point that they usually identify is to survey what is going on.

What follows is a suggested programme, spread over five weeks, for just such an initiative.

Week 1 You are going to assess your own classroom.
Week 2 You are going to make a record of the kinds of reading your class has been doing recently.
Week 3 You are going to give serious thought to the kinds of writing your class has been engaged in.
Week 4 You are going to consider the kinds of oral work you have organized in class.
Week 5 You will summarize your findings against a suggested language policy.

Week 1: the classroom

What overall impression do you gain from looking at the room? In what way can it be called a stimulating language environment?

Do displays and pieces of children's writing suggest that you attach a genuine value to language work? Are the examples of children's writing and drawing recently done? And are the pieces of writing varied? How many children have had no work on display in the past month? And how many have? Are there any examples of group writing, class booklets and the like? Are all of the items on display worthy of being displayed? Do they make a distinct contribution to the language environment? Or are they just pretty bits of paper?

How are tables and chairs arranged? Is there a reason for their present arrangement? Does it have any advantage for children's learning? Did you make the choice on educational grounds, or because you had a vague idea that it was not good to be either trendy or old-fashioned? What disadvantages are there with the present arrangement?

How many books are there in the book corner or in shelves in the room? How many of these are poetry? How many are fiction? How many are non-fiction? How many have you read? Are they all appropriate, or are some too old or too young? Are there some which are never borrowed? Are there some which are dirty or dog-eared? Can you give any sound justification for not burning them? Are there any unworthy of being offered as presents? Do you think you can burn these as well? Do you have a willing caretaker and a can of petrol?!

Can you have a look at your desk? Can you just jot down the titles of the five anthologies which you keep there and from which you read to the children for a few minutes each day?

Do you have any other observations about the room as a language environment?

Week 2: reading

How often do you read aloud to the pupils? Do you read to them for at least a twenty-minute stretch each day? Can you write down what stories and poems you have read aloud to them in the past four weeks?

Does every pupil have a personal reading book at the moment? When and where and for how long does she or he read it in school? Is there time each day for sustained silent reading for pleasure? Do you or the children keep a record of this personal reading? Do you believe that the way to improve reading competence and to enhance children's pleasure in reading is to talk to them individually about what they have read so far, about what they think may happen next, about their feelings towards the story and the people in it?

Is a shared class reader or a group story a regular feature? How are these selected? Are they always successful? What determines success of failure? How do you get children to respond to stories? Do they draw, write and model?

Which poetry books do children voluntarily read? How often do you use a poem as a stimulus for other work? Is this effective? Have you found Sandy Brownjohn's books helpful?

Can you just write down the titles of four children's novels you have read at home in the past two months?

Week 3: writing

Taking all of the writing that six children have done over the past four weeks, can you make a list of the kinds of written activity which they have been involved in? How much writing have they done? How many pages? How much time does this represent? What kinds of writing have they been asked for? Is there a great variety? For instance, in addition to stories and accounts of events, what other kinds of writing have they done? On how many occasions was there any writing for a genuine reason? What was this? Who apart from yourself has the writing been aimed at? How many pieces have been read and commented upon by other people? (Pupils, elder sisters and brothers, parents, other adults? . . .)

Were there many formal exercises in contrast to other kinds of writing? Were these set to respond to particular needs at a particular time or did everyone do the same exercises? As a result of each exercise, are you satisfied that the point you sought to make or the error you aimed to eliminate has been effectively dealt with?

When pupils write do you always respond within two days? And how do you respond? How often do you give a numerical assessment? Can you find a piece of continuous writing marked numerically and say precisely what the numbers (e.g. 6/10) represent? And if you have a letter grade, can you say again what that means? If against a piece of writing you have put no more than a tick, can you explain its significance?

Week 4: oral work

How often is the oral work in your classroom productive? How do you ensure that every pupil has the chance to contribute? Do you have class or small group discussions? Can you list the next five occasions on which pupils are to engage in productive oral work? Are there children to whom you have not spoken in the past fortnight in an informal manner for a period of, say, ten minutes?

Week 5: the moment of truth

Over the past four weeks you have had the opportunity to look at your own work. Now is the time to sum up the experience. What follows is a series of statements against which to test your own thinking:

1 The classroom
   Your classroom should be capable of being described as being a stimulating language environment. In such an environment one would look for:
   - a variety of children's work – writing, models, art – on display
   - work of genuine quality, worthy of display and well displayed
   - tables and chairs arranged so that the best educational results can be achieved

- the books – fiction, poetry, non-fiction – will be appropriate, in good condition, of good quality and varied.

2 Reading

Your policy, which is designed to promote an enjoyment of reading, will include such features as:

- an environment reflecting a concern for books and offering a wide range of reading to children
- daily opportunities for sustained silent reading of books and offering a wide range of reading to children
- daily opportunities for children to hear you read from a range of books including poetry (serious as well as comic!)
- opportunities for children through their classroom work to share literary experiences.

3 Writing

Your approaches to writing will include the following elements:

- writing for a genuine purpose and for a variety of audiences
- writing in a variety of forms
- writing to which you respond in a manner likely to be productive.

4 Oral work

There will be, in the course of any week, many opportunities for children to talk to each other and to adults. You will have well-thought-out strategies which enable children to use their own language to learn.

The next step

First of all, discuss what you have found with your headteacher, or with an adviser, after which it is time to engage one or two of your colleagues in the exercise. At this stage, it would be best to enlist only friends or volunteers!

You must not allow them to rush through it. Give them the weekly tasks and then discuss the findings with them. Do not feel that you have to offer any judgements; you will not always be able to give answers. Anyway, after the discussion, and only then, give them the next week's sheet.

Make sure that you fix the dates in your diaries in advance: then there's no escape! Your discussions may be best held away from other colleagues, perhaps in the classroom of one of the teachers involved.

Principles of procedure

These are 'bedrock principles' on which you and your colleagues must agree if the language curriculum is to be coherent. It is very important that you not only ensure that the National Curriculum programmes of study are fully covered, but also that you keep clearly in mind those other approaches and activities which you know from experience benefit the children in your classes.

These principles are not closed like aims and objectives but are 'open'. For example:

Objective: At the end of year 3, children should be able to use speech marks.
Principles of procedure: Every child should have the opportunity to use her or his own language to make sense of experiences in school.

1 Draw up a list of these bedrock principles, bearing in mind all of the areas of language experience: talking, writing, reading and listening.
2 What are the classroom implications of your principles? For example, if every child should have the opportunity to use her or his own language to make sense of experience, are whole class discussions where only four or five children contribute valid? If not, what other strategies are available?

The language policy document

It is not unlikely that the recently appointed language co-ordinator will be pressed to produce a policy statement, or modify an existing document. The process of drafting such a statement is extremely useful but will take a long time! Indeed, there is a convincing argument which says that the process never stops since the policy, if it is any good, must develop and grow. The policy must reflect what happens in the classroom as well as what it is hoped will happen.

A language policy document might include:

- A statement of principles of procedure of the kind we looked at earlier. This would identify the style of learning the school wishes to underpin its language development work.
- Suggestions of successful learning/teaching strategies and how they were set up.
- Examples of children's work and teacher-produced booklets, worksheets and so on.
- How to plan for progression and continuity.
- The evaluation of the policy in practice.
- The criteria used for the selection of resources.
- The concepts, skills and attitudes which are to be developed.
- How children's progress is to be monitored and assessed.
- Key learning experiences planned for pupils.
- Lists of resources and addresses and so on.
- Important articles from journals or extracts from books.
- Policy statements on issues like:
  - the library
  - multi-cultural education
  - what children should know about language
  - drama
  - media education
  - etc.

The document may not therefore take the form of the conventional stapled booklet but might be contained in a large ring binder or folder with clear plastic envelopes. In this way it is hoped that, as the school's thinking develops and changes, so will the policy. It is also very important that if possible the whole staff should be involved in the drafting and compiling of this document in some way. It should not be seen as the job of the language co-ordinator operating in isolation.

Planning

The starting point for the planning of the primary language curriculum is not merely located around a discussion about different kinds of content but is more concerned with the question 'What do I want the children to learn from the sequence of work I am offering?' Any really useful planning tool will, of course, also have built into it an evaluative element and guidance relating to assessment in both the formative and summative senses.

It is important therefore to be clear about the:

- Concepts: what we want the children to understand.
- Competences: what we want the children to do.
- Knowledge: what we want the children to know.
- Outcomes: what kind of things will the children produce and who will be the audience(s) for these?

Also how you intend to achieve these by considering where you will start, what resources you will need, how you will organize the children, how long you anticipate the sequence of work will last and what styles of learning the children will be involved in.

Once the work is complete and you have decided what worked well and what could be improved next time you are in a position to decide where to place the emphasis on the next sequence of work.

One teacher of KS2 children who wished to deliver the National Curriculum history core study unit on Britain since 1930 and to link this work with the Economic and Industrial Understanding cross-curricular theme (EIU) used this framework devised by teachers in the North London Language Consortium. This is described in the following case study.

Case study 1: history and economic and industrial understanding at KS2[2]

Within the history programme of study on Britain since 1930 aspects of social and cultural changes were focused upon. It was felt that the 'skills, attitudes and knowledge' outlined in the EIU document would support the development and teaching of historical skills and understanding as specified in the orders for history.

Having identified that we wanted to link history and EIU together we asked ourselves: What do we want the children to be able to do, know and understand?

We wanted the children *historically*:

In terms of *language* we wanted the children to:

- to understand (concepts):
  - differences between past and present times
  - how to make deductions from a range of historical sources
  - a variety of different features of a historical period.
- to be able to (competences):
  - use and handle a range of artefacts
  - communicate their information in a variety of ways
  - create their own museum
  - work collaboratively.
- to know (knowledge):
  - about cultural and social changes including changes in fashion, music, toys and everyday life from 1930
  - how historical artefacts help to explain changes in the roles of people, and family life over time.

From an *EIU* perspective we wanted the children to:

- know and understand:
  - the different roles of individuals they have met and observed at work in a local museum
  - understand the different nature of work – some is paid, other work voluntary
  - to make decisions about the use of resources
  - about a public service in their local community.
- be able to:
  - collect, analyse and interpret data
  - make economic decisions
  - show an interest in people and places in the local community.

We decided that the learning outcome was for the children to design and produce a museum of Britain since 1930 from historical artefacts, photographs, adverts, etc. which either they, the staff or local community would provide. Hence a letter was written by the children and sent to all parents, governors and selected members of the local community in advance of starting the project to ask for a range of artefacts to be loaned to the school for their museum.

The children then had to consider who the museum would be for. By deciding they wanted to invite grandparents, senior citizens from the nearby day centre, pupils, staff, their parents, governors and local museum curators, they had to plan carefully how they would put the museum together in order to meet the different needs of those who would visit their museum.

The starting point for this project was a visit to the local museum. On their visit the children, with support from the museum staff, looked carefully and critically at the ways in which the museum presented the artefacts, paintings, etc. and the ways in which the museum raised money.

Although this work includes references to a range of language activities its main focus is historical. What would this planning sheet look like if the learning intentions were language centred?

Finally

We want to place an emphasis on the need for sustained evaluation of what is going on by everyone involved. Obviously, we do not exclude the children themselves from this process, and the last section of this chapter focuses on the insights children have, and the contribution they can therefore make, to the developing language and learning policy of the school.

One startlingly obvious way is actually to talk with children about how effectively they think they have been learning. We included some material on this in Chapter 2, 'Speaking and listening'. Another approach is to employ a learning journal or learning log. Our second case study in Chapter 3, 'Writing', has already mentioned this briefly, but we now wish to focus on the particular contribution such an approach can make.

> The trouble with asking a teacher for help is that they always go right back to the beginning when they explain, when really it's only one little bit you didn't get.
>
> Kirsty, aged 9½

A learning journal is a notebook in which the child writes her or his own reflections on the learning experiences in which she or he has been involved. This may go some way to solving Kirsty's problem in so far as the writer focuses precisely on the particular issue which is causing problems. It is interesting to note that sometimes it is through the writing of the problem that the problem is resolved. It underlines our earlier emphasis on writing as a learning and thinking process.

The teacher responds to the entry in the journal and is able to give specific help or guidance.

How to set up learning journals:

1 Discuss the idea fully with your headteacher.
2 Do not 'mark' the journal entries for technical blemishes. The idea is that you are interested in what the child says, not how technically correct it is.

Interestingly, teachers have noted that once this pressure is removed, the quality of the writing in the journal is higher than the writing produced in more formal and conventional contexts.

3 Make sure that the children know it is only the learning which takes place in your classrooms that you are interested in and can comment on. This usually avoids the possibility of adverse (or otherwise!) comment on colleagues.

4 Keep the journal confidential. This is very important because it builds up the confidence of the writer and sharpens the sense of a specific audience: the teacher as trusted adult. Only show journals to colleagues if you have the permission of the individual writer.

The journal is one way of finding out what children take from their learning experiences, and it also encourages them to take a greater responsibility for their own learning. Furthermore, journals can form a basis for genuine negotiation between the teacher and the children about what they do next – and how.

The topic based cross-curricular approach commonly adopted in primary school classrooms can offer a useful vehicle for promoting children's language development . . . we need to plan our learning activities very carefully – language is too important to be left to chance.

East Sussex Curriculum Guidelines For Primary Language

12 Making sense of it all

Campsbourne Infant School: Required for September 1982, a part-time (0.5) teacher whose role will be co-ordinating language and literacy work throughout the school, running the resource room, library and mothers and toddlers group, doing group work, making materials and supporting other members of staff. Salary scale 1.
Making sense of it all

From a Haringey LEA notice about part-time
teaching vacancies[1]

How good a language co-ordinator do you think you are?

Check your answers (see pp. 111–12) with:

Check your answers (see pp. 111–12) with:

- your headteacher
- a colleague.

1 SPEAKING AND LISTENING

(i) The headteacher invites Dr Boris from the local polytechnic to give a lecture to the staff about 'Talk'.

Do you:

(a) Breathe a sigh of relief that the next staff meeting is not your responsibility?
(b) Contact Dr Boris urgently and persuade her as to the kind of participatory session you want?
(c) Boycott the meeting?
(d) Discuss with the headteacher how the meeting can best fit the needs of the staff?

(ii) One member of staff dismisses 'talk' as 'pointless chatter'.

Do you:

(a) Ignore her and get on with other aspects of your job?
(b) Hand her a copy of the National Curriculum Programmes of Study?
(c) Suggest that you go on a course together?

(d) Lend her a tape-recorder?

(e) Manoeuvre a situation where you can teach together?

(iii) You are confronted with a colleague who claims, in scathing terms, that 'children never listen nowadays'.

Do you:

(a) Not listen?

(b) Argue passionately that children need to be motivated to listen?

(c) Agree smilingly and assume it is inevitable that some colleagues simply cannot cope?

(d) Tell the headteacher?

(e) Listen; remember, and later on suggest a mutual activity where evaluation of talking and listening in your respective classrooms is essential?

2 WRITING

(i) The head asks you to review the policy for 'creative writing'.

Do you:

(a) Refuse?

(b) Ask him or her what 'creative' means?

(c) Ask staff to let you have some examples of children's writing from their classes?

(d) Photocopy the policy, place it in staff pigeon-holes and ask for comment?

(e) Look at a specific aspect – drafting, for example, or 'finding an audience'?

(ii) An Inspector on the point of leaving the school after a day's visit, comments that children in the school 'write too much narrative to the exclusion of other genres'.

Do you:

(a) Giggle and say 'Eh?'

(b) Stop her/him leaving and ask for time to discuss the matter?

(c) Make a point of taking a cross-section sample from all colleagues of pupil writing over a period of time to see if the comment is valid?

(d) Ignore it?

(e) Look at your own practice over the past week to gauge the range of writing opportunities children have had?

(iii) A parent of a top junior girl shows you a piece of writing in which you have failed to correct 'I have wrote a story'.

Do you:

(a) Apologize?

(b) Say you were tired when you marked it?

(c) Tell her that you always discuss such matters with the child rather than overdo the red pen?

(d) Emphasize the importance of 'creativity'?

(e) Point out the good things in the piece and evade the question?

3 READING

(i) Currently, parents are not involved in the school's reading policy.

Do you:

(a) Call a large meeting of parents and outline their role in their new policy?

(b) Keep it like that?

(c) Review the reading policy, involving all the staff?

(d) Institute a 'a parents-in-partnership' scheme with your own class?

(e) Send a letter to parents stressing how important their role is in developing reading?

(ii) The school library is fragmented throughout the school: each class has its own library and there is a separate centre for non-book resources.

Do you:

(a) Abolish class libraries?

(b) Ask for the advice of the LEA Education Library Service?

(c) Review as a staff, the school's library policy?

(d) Keep it like that?

(e) Monitor library use over a period of time?

(iii) A handful of parents, the head (and you!) believe in 'real' books for real readers, picture books rather than the dated reading scheme you have inherited. The other five members of staff are not so keen, indeed three are very hostile.

Do you:

(a) Seize *The Times Educational Supplement* with mounting passion every Friday?

(b) Attempt to increase the 'handful' of parents to a vociferous lobby?

(c) Bide your time and emphasize the importance of a range of approaches to the teaching of reading?

(d) Manoeuvre things so that in the earlier years you can shift towards 'real' books?

(e) Not buy any more of the existing reading scheme; 'steal' copies occasionally and 'lose' them?!

4 DRAMA

The local comprehensive asks you to agree to the school being used as a venue for a competitive festival which the secondary head of drama department has dreamed up. Liaison hitherto has been non-existent.

Do you:

(a) Agree and let them get on with it?
(b) Refuse?
(c) Suggest an alternative date and an organizing committee?
(d) Ask the head to make a decision?

5 MICROS

A local computer firm offers you an out-of-date micro that is not compatible with your Archimedes machines.

Do you:

(a) Turn it down?
(b) Accept graciously?
(c) Accept and then try to sell it?
(d) Ring the adviser (if he's not too busy inspecting) and ask for help?

6 LIAISON

The local comprehensive, with whom you have tenuous links, asks you, along with other 'feeder' schools, to administer a new format for recording pupil progress in the final term. It does not fit easily with your current policy.

Do you:

(a) Write back offering to convene an exploratory meeting mentioning the existence of the National Curriculum?
(b) Send back a written rationale for your current position on testing?
(c) Ignore it?
(d) Write 'Not known at this address' and return it?

7 THE HEAD

The newly appointed head does not like the rather *laissez-faire* policy on evaluation in the school. She asks you to provide a detailed breakdown of specific language issues that the school needs to address.

Do you:

(a) Feel threatened?
(b) Groan and get on with it?

(c) Welcome the new head's positive approach?

(d) Scribble down, without real evaluation, issues that you know the school should focus on?

How good a language co-ordinator? The 'answers'

1 SPEAKING AND LISTENING

(i)	(ii)	(iii)
(a) = 0	(a) = 4	(a) = 0
(b) = 4	(b) = 0	(b) = 2
(c) = 2	(c) = 1	(c) = 1
(d) = 2	(d) = 2	(d) = 1
	(e) = 3	(e) = 3

2 WRITING

(i)	(ii)	(iii)
(a) = 0	(a) = 0	(a) = 0
(b) = 2	(b) = 1	(b) = 1
(c) = 1	(c) = 2	(c) = 3
(d) = 2	(d) = 0	(d) = 2
(e) = 3	(e) = 3	(e) = 2

3 READING

(i)	(ii)	(iii)
(a) = 0	(a) = 0	(a) = 1
(b) = 0	(b) = 2	(b) = 2
(c) = 4	(c) = 3	(c) = 2
(d) = 3	(d) = 0	(d) = 4
(e) = 1	(e) = 3	(e) = 3

4 DRAMA

(a) = 1
(b) = 2
(c) = 4
(d) = 3

5 MICROS

(a) = 1
(b) = 2
(c) = 3
(d) = 4

6 LIAISON

> (a) = 4
> (b) = 2
> (c) = 1
> (d) = 3

7 THE HEAD

> (a) = 1
> (b) = 3
> (c) = 4
> (d) = 2

How did you do?

- If you scored between 0 and 15 you would be well advised to admit the truth and get out while the going's good. This mark is disgraceful!
- 15–20: A few signs of hope, but in the main your heart is not in this. It is a surprise that you bought this book. Would you be happier in charge of Road Safety?
- 20–25: You are qualified for the job, but there are worrying signs of rustiness, or is it perverse stubbornness? You should consider a long secondment, an OU course or confident applications for headship.
- 25–30: You show a promising flair for the job, but you should take a firmer, more assertive stance on such issues. Smile less and argue more. Perhaps you should join a firm of management consultants!
- 30–35: You almost have what it takes. Have you thought seriously about joining the National Curriculum Council?
- 35+: You are extraordinarily talented and very underpaid. You could organize anyone or anything and I would, hesitatingly, suggest a career in politics.

Finally

A child should learn to do the following in any satisfactory language environment:

ask questions
answer questions
discuss possible actions
explain
become critical of own work
become critical of other's work
talk to gain agreement
search for solutions

suggest
be tentative
record
transpose information
list
classify
define
label
compose poems
expand sentences
make notes
keep logs
record responses to a story
reshape incidents
adopt roles
see other viewpoints
read instructions
listen to instructions
give instructions
read aloud
read silently
report
solve problems
listen to stories
control own behaviour
relate to others
make hypotheses
analyse
describe
reflect on experience
demonstrate understanding
extend learning
find information
select information
adapt to an audience
make decisions
co-operate
draft, redraft and edit
choose a book
complete a book
narrate (orally and in writing)
write letters
review
take responsibility
spell
punctuate
question
comment on

predict
check
use word processor
set problems[2]

Are there more?!

Appendix I
Books about language

Background texts

Barnes, D., *From Communication to Curriculum*, Harmondsworth: Penguin, 1976.
Britton, J., *Language and Learning*, Harmondsworth: Penguin, 1970.
DES, *A Language for Life*, London: HMSO, 1975.
DES, *English for Ages 5 to 16*, London: HMSO, June 1989.
DES, *National Curriculum: From Policy to Practice*, London: HMSO, 1989.
Edwards, D. and Mercer, N., *Common Knowledge*, London: Methuen, 1987.
NCC, *A Framework for the Primary Curriculum* (Curriculum guidance series No. 1), York, 1989.
Smith, F., *Joining the Literacy Club*, Reading: Centre for the Teaching of Reading, 1984, in conjunction with the Abel Press.
Wells, G., *Learning through Interaction*, Cambridge: Cambridge University Press, 1981.
Wells, G., *Language, Learning and Education*, Walton-on-Thames: NFER/Nelson, 1985.

About talk

Folker, A. and Coles, M., *Children Talking*, Learning about Learning Booklet No. 5, Wiltshire Education Dept.
Goff, P., 'The effects of talking on writing', *English in Education*, Autumn 1979.
Howe, A., *Expanding Horizons*, Sheffield: NATE, 1988.
Lewis, R., 'Talking in the middle school', *English in Education*, Spring 1978.
MacLure, M. and Hargreaves, M., *Speaking and Listening Assessment at Age 11*, Walton-on-Thames: NFER/Nelson, 1986.
Martin, N. *et al.*, *Understanding Children Talking*, Harmondsworth: Penguin, 1976.
National Oracy Project, *Learning Together Through Talk: Key Stages 1 and 2*, London: Hodder & Stoughton, 1992.
National Oracy Project, *Thinking Voices* (NOP reader), London: Hodder & Stoughton, 1992.
Wilkinson, A. *et al.*, *Spoken English Illuminated*, Milton Keynes: Open University Press, 1990.

Writing

Beard, R., *Children's Writing in the Primary School*, London: Hodder & Stoughton, 1984.
D'Arcy, P., *Making Sense, Shaping Meaning*, London: Heinemann/Boynton Cook, 1989.
Dougill, P. and Hackman, S., *Frameworks for Writing*, London: Macmillan, 1987.
Graves, D., *Writing: Teachers and Children at Work*, London: Heinemann, 1983.
HMI, *Aspects of Writing in English in the Junior School*, London: HMI, 1987.
Kress, G., *Learning to Write*, London: Routledge & Kegan Paul, 1982.
Perera, K., *Children's Writing and Reading*, Oxford: Basil Blackwell, 1984.
Raban, B. (ed.), *Practical Ways to Teach Writing*, London: Ward Lock Educational, 1985.
Smith, F., *Writing and the Writer*, London: Heinemann, 1982.
Smith, F., *Reading like a Writer*, Reading: Centre for the Teaching of Reading, 1984, in conjunction with the Abel Press.
White, J., *The Assessment of Writing Pupils Aged 11 and 15*, Walton-on-Thames: NFER/Nelson, 1986.
Wilkinson, A., *The Writing of Writing*, Milton Keynes: Open University Press, 1986.

Micros and language

Broderick, C. and Trushell, J., 'Problems and processes', *English in Education*, Summer 1985.
Chandler, D., 'Why we don't need word-processors . . . yet', *NATENEWS*, Summer 1986.
Chandler, D. and Marcus, S., *Computers and Literacy*, Milton Keynes: Open University Press, 1985.
NATE, *IT's English: Accessing English With Computers*, Sheffield: NATE, 1990.
National Council for Educational Technology, *Primary Language: Extending the Primary Curriculum with Computers*, London: NCET, 1991.
National Writing Project, *Writing and Micros*, London: Nelson, 1990.
Raleigh, M., 'Word processing', *English Magazine*, 15.

Poetry

Brownjohn, S., *Does It Have to Rhyme?* London: Hodder & Stoughton, 1980.
Brownjohn, S., *What Rhymes with Secret?* London: Hodder & Stoughton, 1982.
Corbett, P. and Moses, B., *Catapults and Kingfishers: Teaching Poetry in Primary Schools*, Oxford, Oxford University Press, 1986.
Dunn, J., Styles, M. and Warburton, N., *In Tune With Yourself*, Cambridge: Cambridge University Press, 1987.
Merrick, B., *Exploring Poetry: 9–13*. Sheffield: NATE, 1991.
Styles, M. and Triggs, P., *Poetry 0–16*, London: Books for Keeps, 1988.

Reading

Barrs *et al.*, *The Reading Book*, London: CPLE, 1991.
Bennett, J., *Learning to Read with Picture Books* (4th edn), Stroud: Thimble, 1991.
Benton, M. and Fox, G., *Teaching Literature, 9 to 14*, Oxford: Oxford University Press, 1985.

Butler, D., *Cushla and Her Books*, London: Hodder & Stoughton, 1979.

Chambers, A., *Booktalk*, London: Bodley Head, 1985.

Devon Education, *A Devon Approach to Book Provision in Primary Schools*, Devon LEA, 1992.

Dombey, H. *et al.*, *On the Teaching of Reading*, Brighton: The Literacy Centre, University of Brighton, 1991.

Graham, J., *Pictures On the Page*, Sheffield: NATE, 1991.

Heeks, P., *Choosing and Using Books in the First School*, London: Macmillan, 1981.

Ingham, J., *Books and Reading Development*, London: Heinemann, 1981.

Lunzer, E. and Gardner, K., *The Effective Use of Reading*, London: Heinemann, 1984.

Meek, M., *How Texts Teach What Children Learn*, Stroud: Thimble Press, 1988.

Meek, M., *On Being Literate*, London: Bodley Head, 1991.

Moon, C. (ed.), *Practical Ways to Teach: Reading*, London: Ward Lock Educational.

NATE Primary Committee, *Children Reading to Their Teachers*, Sheffield: NATE, undated.

Pumphrey, P., *Improving Children's Reading in the Junior School: Challenges and Responses*, London: Cassell, 1991.

Smith, F., *Reading* (2nd edn), Cambridge: Cambridge University Press, 1985.

Southgate, V., Arnold, H. and Johnson, S., *Extending Beginning Reading*, London: Heinemann, 1981.

Wade, B., *Reading for Real*, Milton Keynes: Open University Press, 1989.

Wallen, M. (ed.), *Every Picture Tells . . .*, Sheffield: NATE, 1990.

Wray, D. (ed.), *Standards in Reading*, Perspectives 44, Exeter: School of Education, University of Exeter, 1991.

Knowledge about language

Carter, R. (ed.), *Knowledge about Language in the Curriculum: The LINC Reader*, London: Hodder and Stoughton, 1991.

Harris, J. and Wilkinson, J. (eds), *A Guide to English Language in the National Curriculum*, Cheltenham: Stanley Thornes, 1990.

Hawkins, E., *Awareness of Language: An Introduction*, Cambridge: Cambridge University Press, 1984.

Jones, M. and West, A. (eds), *Learning Me Your Language*, London: Mary Glasgow, 1988.

Mittins, B., *English: Not the Naming of Parts*, Sheffield: NATE, 1988.

Mittins, B., *Language Awareness for Teachers*, Milton Keynes: Open University Press, 1990.

Perera, K., *Understanding Language*, National Association of Advisers for English, 1987.

Media Education

Bazalgette, C., *Media Education*, London: Hodder and Stoughton, 1991.

Bazalgette, C. (ed.), *Primary Media Education a Curriculum Statement*, London: BFI/DES BFI Education, 1989.

Buckingham, D. (ed.), *Watching Media Learning*, London: Falmer Press, 1990.

Fox, K. and Bennion, S., *Story to Story Language Development through Media Education*, Southampton: TVS Education, 1991.

Masterman, L., *Teaching about Television*, London: Macmillan, 1980.

Masterman, L., *Teaching the Media*, London: Comedia, 1985.

Drama

Bolton, G., *Towards a Theory of Drama in Education*, London: Longman, 1979.

Bolton, G., *Selected Writings: Gavin Bolton on Drama in Education*, London: Longman, 1986.

Brandes, D. and Phillips, H., *Gamester's Handbook 1*, London: Hutchinson, 1978.

Brandes, D., *Gamester's Handbook 2*, London: Hutchinson, 1982.

Davies, G., *Practical Primary Drama*, London: Heinemann, 1983.

Johnson, L. and O'Neill, C. (eds), *Dorothy Heathcote: Collected Writings on Education and Drama*, London: Hutchinson, 1984.

Neelands, J., *Making Sense of Drama*, London: Heinemann, 1984.

O'Neill, C. and Lambert, A., *Drama Structures*, London: Hutchinson, 1982.

Wakefield LEA, *Some Uses of Role-Play as an Approach to the Study of Fiction, 8–14*, Wakefield.

Others

Alexander, R., Rose, J. and Woodhead, C., *Curriculum Organisation and Classroom Practice in Primary Schools*, London: DES, 1992.

Barrs, M. *et al.*, *The Primary Language Record*, London: CPLE, 1991.

Barrs, M. *et al.*, *Pattens of Learning*, London: CPLE.

Blenkin, G. and Kelly, A. V., *The Primary Curriculum: A Process Approach to Curriculum Planning*, London: Harper & Row, 1987.

Bruner, J. S., *Actual Minds, Possible Worlds*, London: Harvard University Press, 1986.

Open University, *Every Child's Language: An In-service Pack for Primary Teachers*, Course P534, Milton Keynes: Open University LMSO, 1985.

Schools Council, *Primary Practice*, Schools Council Working Paper 75, London: Methuen, 1983.

Appendix II
Where to find things out

Books for Keeps, published by the School Bookshop Association, 1 Effingham Road, Lee, London SE12 8NZ.

Books for Keeps' Guide to Children's Books for a Multi-cultural Society 0–7.

Books for Keeps' Guide to Children's Books for a Multi-cultural Society 8 to 12.

Bookquest, published by the University of Brighton Literacy Centre, Falmer, East Sussex; teacher reviews with a primary emphasis; occasional feature articles or interviews.

The Directory of Curriculum Development and In-Service Training Providers, Grapevine Education, P.O. Box 1356, Worthing, West Sussex BN13 IQ3

NATENEWS, newsletter of the National Association for the Teaching of English.

Signal Bookguides, Thimble Press, Lockwood Station Rd, South Woodchester, Stroud, Gloucestershire.

Useful addresses

British Film Institute (BFI), 21 Stephen Street, London W1P 1PL.

Centre for Language in Primary Education, London Borough of Southwark, Webber Row, London SE1 8QW.

Centre for the Teaching of Reading, University of Reading, Reading, Berkshire.

English and Media Centre, 136 Chalton Street, London NW1 1RX.

MOMI Education, Museum of the Moving Image, South Bank, London SE1 8XT.

NAPE (National Association for Primary Education), 4 Chequers Place, Headington Quarry, Oxford.

NATE (National Association for the Teaching of English), 50 Broadfield Rd, Broadfield Business Centre, Sheffield S8 0XJ.

Schools Poetry Association, c/o Twyford School, Winchester, Hampshire.

United Kingdom Reading Association (UKRA), c/o Edge Hill College of Education, St Helens Road, Ormskirk, Lancashire.

Writers in schools

The Writers in Schools scheme, run by your local Regional Arts Association (RAA), is designed to make it easier for you to invite in professional writers to work in your school. Normally, the RAA publishes a directory of such writers and subsidizes the visit (about half, plus travel).

Notes

1 What should the post-holder do?

1 From 'A life in the day of Daniel Harvey', *Sunday Times*, 23 June 1985. At the time Daniel was 9 and at school in Newcastle.

2 Speaking and listening

1 Gene Kemp, *Charlie Lewis Plays for Time* (London: Faber & Faber, 1984).
2 James Britton, *Language and Learning* (Harmondsworth: Penguin, 1970), p. 223.
3 From 'National Trust' in Tony Harrison, *Selected Poems* (Harmondsworth: Penguin, 1984), p. 121.
4 I am indebted to David Allen, English Inspector in Nottinghamshire, for these statements.
5 DES, *English from 5 to 16: Curriculum Matters 1* (London: DES, 1984).
6 DES, *English from 5 to 16: The Responses to Curriculum Matters 1* (London: DES, 1986).
7 Converse confidently and pleasantly in social situations (the age specified in *English from 5 to 16* is 11).
  Describe clearly experiences they have undergone (16).
  Make clear statements of fact (11).
  Frame pertinent questions (11).
  Explain what they are doing when involved in a task (7).
  Speak in role in dramatic play (7).
  Make and take telephone calls, giving and receiving information accurately (16).
  Argue a case (16).
  Express ideas and feelings accurately (11).
  Describe what they have observed (7).
  Use the resources of the voice (modulation, tone, etc.) expressively (16).
  Use gesture and movement in association with the voice when effective communication demands it (7).
  Give short talks on matters of which they have knowledge (16).
8 Frank Smith, *Joining the Literacy Club* (Reading: Centre for the Teaching of Reading/Abel Press, 1984).
9 Ibid., p. 5.

10 I am grateful to Mrs Oonagh Cox for this transcript.

11 *English from 5 to 16: The Responses*, p. 13.

12 For an interesting account of a drama teacher planning for meaningful contexts, see Dorothy Heathcote, 'Drama as context for talking and writing' in *Dorothy Heathcote: Collected Writings on Education and Drama*, ed. L. Johnson and C. O'Neill (London: Hutchinson, 1984).

13 For other suggestions here see *Primary Practice*, Schools Council Working Paper 75 (London: Methuen Educational, 1983), pp. 57–8.

14 A phrase borrowed from Alan Howe, Director of the Wiltshire Oracy Project.

15 In *Children Talking* by Andrew Folker and Martin Coles, one of Wiltshire Education Department's 'Learning about Learning' booklets (no. 5).

16 F. P. Heide, *The Shrinking of Treehorn* (London: Puffin, 1975).

17 *Oracy Matters* is the newsletter of the Wiltshire Oracy Project, April 1985.

18 I am indebted to Steve Cooper for this example.

19 From 'Dawn reads to her teacher' by Anne Baker, one of the articles in *Children Reading to Their Teachers* (Sheffield: NATE, 1984).

20 E. B. White, *Charlotte's Web* (London: Puffin, 1963).

21 I am again grateful to Oonagh Cox for this material.

22 Connie Rosen, quoted by Roger Lewis in *English in Education*, Spring 1978.

23 *English from 5 to 16*.

24 Andrew Wilkinson, *The Foundations of Language* (Oxford, 1971).

25 HMI, *Education 8 to 12 in Combined Middle Schools* (London: DES, 1985), p. 5.

26 Broadcast in *English Now* on BBC Radio 4, 4 June 1984.

27 *Selected Poems*, p. 109.

28 E. P. Thompson, *The Making of the English Working Class* (Harmondsworth: Penguin, 1970).

29 I am indebted to Alan Howe for drawing my attention to the work of Garth Boomer upon which this section is based.

30 I would like to thank Ken Wilby for drawing my attention to the work on Jigsaw going on in a number of Hampshire schools including Copner Middle School, Portsmouth where Jane Locke and her colleagues worked with children in Y4 and Y5.

31 Dave Cath at Kennet School, Thatcham, Berkshire, produced this document as part of a project initiated by Southern Conference for Development Work in English.

3 Writing

1 Tony Harrison, *Selected Poems* (Harmondsworth: Penguin, 1984), p. 112.

2 Ibid., p. 121.

3 Margaret Drabble, *Arnold Bennett* (London: Futura, 1975).

4 Donald Graves, *Writing: Teachers and Children at Work* (London: Heinemann, 1983).

5 From Gareth Owen, *Song of the City* (London: Fontana Young Lions Original, 1985).

6 The extracts are taken from the following sources:

   (A) Anne Baker in *Real Writing, Real Readers: A Question of Choice*, from an article in 'English in Education' (NATE)

   (B) *English in Berkshire Schools*, Curriculum guidelines 5–16. (Response to DES Circular 6/81.)

   (C) *Stimulus for Writing: Literacy, Language and Writing*.

(D) Mary Hoffman, *Reading, Writing and Relevance* (London: Hodder & Stoughton, 1976).
(E) Geoffrey Thornton in an article for the National Association of English Advisers on the APU Language Monitoring.
(F) Teach Writing as a Process Not a Product
(G) An extract from *The Daily Telegraph*, 3 October 1984, quoted in DES, *English from 5 to 16: The Responses* (London: DES, 1986).
(H) *English from 5 to 16: The Responses.*
(I) Ibid.
(J) DES, *English from 5 to 16: Curriculum Matters 1* (London: DES, 1984).
(K) Cambridgeshire LEA, *English 9–14: Some Guidelines* (Cambridge, 1980).
(L) Frank Smith, *Reading Like a Writer* (Reading: Centre for the Teaching of Reading, 1985).

 7 A phrase borrowed from John Richmond, then English Adviser in Shropshire.
 8 *Writing: Teachers and Children at Work.*
 9 Martin Coles is a member of NAPE and lectures at the School of Educational Studies, University of Portsmouth.
10 *Arnold Bennett*, p. 11.
11 Carolyn Steedman, *The Tidy House* (London: Virago, 1982), p. 99.
12 Jane Doonan, 'About writing', *SCDC National Writing Project Newsletter*, No. 3; Jane Doonan is a teacher in Avon.
13 Doris Lessing.
14 Gene Kemp, *Charlie Lewis Plays for Time* (London: Faber, 1984), p. 47.
15 *Writing: Teachers and Children at Work*
16 A pupil's view (from a school involved in the National Writing Project).
17 James Britton.
18 Jan Mark, *Thunder and Lightnings* (London: Puffin, 1978), p. 35.
19 Seymour Papert, *Mindstorms: Children, Computers and Powerful Ideas* (Brighton: Harvester Press, 1980).
20 David Blake, teacher in charge of language at Earls Barton Junior School, Northampton.
21 This map, particularly the idea of moving from 'pre-writing' to 'composing' and on to 'publishing', draws on Avon's National Writing Project experience as described by the co-ordinator, Richard Bates.
22 English Adviser in Wiltshire.
23 I am grateful to Dee Vickery, Lovelace Primary School, Kingston-upon-Thames, for this case study.
24 Eddie Rigby, Crown Wood School, Bracknell.
25 Bill Agnew in *The Times*, 6 May 1986.
26 *Mindstorms: Children, Computers and Powerful Ideas.*
27 In writing this case study I have drawn on an account by Joan Ashton and Ann Kneen in *Micro Applications in the Teaching of English* (Berkshire LEA, 1986).
28 This INSET video, produced by Mark Chapman, is available from Reading Teachers' Centre.
29 At Dedworth Middle School, Windsor.
30 Available from Shropshire LEA.
31 The following computer programs helped generate this work: EXTRA; FRONT PAGE, MAPE;

FLEET STREET EDITOR, Mirrorsoft; WORDWISE PLUS, Computer Concepts; MICRO-
FAX, Acornsoft (used to write pages of teletext).

32 Michael Clark, 'Young writers and the computer', a paper in *Computers and Literacy*,
ed. D. Chandler and S. Marcus (Milton Keynes: Open University Press, 1985), p. 25.

33 Frank Smith, *Writing and the Writer* (London: Heinemann Educational, 1982), p. 211.

34 The questionnaire is the work of Shropshire teachers involved in the National Writing
Project.

35 Borrowed and adapted from *Writing Development: Suggestions for a Policy 8–13*
(Rotherham LEA). I was reminded of it by Natalie Andrews and Audrey Gregory.

36 Contained in Chris Powling, *Daredevils and Scaredycats* (London: Fontana Lions,
1981).

37 Drawings for the spelling leaflet by Grant Cook.

38 A fuller account of an approach tailored to individual needs is to be found in Jennifer
Hepburn's article, 'Spelling Categories and Strategies', *Reading*, April 1991.

39 HMI, 'Aspects of writing in the Junior School', quoted in *The Times Educational
Supplement*, 6 February 1987.

4 Reading for meaning, for pleasure and for life

1   From *Poetry Matters 4*, Autumn 1986. Also in *Conkers* (Oxford: Oxford University
Press).

2   DES, *A Language for Life* (London: HMSO, 1975), p. 50. Quoted in H. Dombey *et al.*,
On the Teaching of Reading (University of Brighton, 1991).

3   Marie Clay, *Observing Young Readers* (Exeter NH: Heinemann, 1982).

4   From Angel Scott, 'What is a Reader?', *NATENEWS*, the bulletin of the National
Association for the Teaching of English, Autumn 1985.

5   Gene Kemp, *Charlie Lewis Plays for Time* (London: Faber & Faber, 1984), pp. 46–7.

6   Barrie Wade, 'Reading Rickets and the Uses of Story', *English in Education* 16 (3).

7   From *The Guardian*, 16 September 1986.

8   *Readers and Texts 1: The Reading Process*, compiled and edited by Bob Moy for the
English Centre (London: ILEA, 1980).

9   I am grateful to Henrietta Dombey for the progress in reading questions.

10 Open University, *Children, Language and Literature*, Course P530 (Milton Keynes:
Open University LMSO, 1982).

11 I am grateful to Chris Vallance for this case study.

12 This case study was written by D. A. Froggatt, Chesworth Junior School, Horsham.

13 For more on DARTS, see E. Lunzer and K. Gardner (eds) *The Effective Use of Reading*
(London: Heinemann, 1979) and E. Lunzer and K. Gardner (eds) *Learning from the
Written Word* (Edinburgh: Oliver & Boyd, 1984). A complementary approach to
reading for information is described in Jennifer E. Eden's article, 'Helping Pupils to
Read for Information', *Reading*, July 1991.

14 Quoted by Wendy Cope, *Making Cocoa for Kingsley Amis* (London: Faber, 1986). It
came originally from an interview in *The Guardian*.

15 Quoted in DES, *Teaching Poetry in the Secondary School: An HMI View* (London:
HMSO, 1987).

16 Brian Powell, *English through Poetry Writing* (London: Heinemann, 1968).

17 Sandy Brownjohn's books are referred to in Appendix I. 'Thirty-six things to do with a
poem' can be found in *Children, Language and Literature*.

18 *Better School Libraries in Primary Schools* (National Association of Advisers in English, 1985).

5 Media education

1 I am grateful to Julian Bowker for his invaluable assistance in writing this chapter.
2 UNESCO Declaration on Media Education, 1982.
3 Len Masterman, *Teaching the Media* (London: Comedia, 1985).
4 See pp. 42–3.
5 *The Observer*, 5 April 1987.

6 Drama for learning

1 I am grateful to Kate Fleming for her contribution to this section.
2 ILEA, *Drama Guidelines* (London: ILEA/Heinemann, 1976).
3 Ibid., p. 9.
4 Dorothy Heathcote, 'Drama and Learning', L. Johnson and C. O'Neill (eds), *Dorothy Heathcote: Collected Writings on Education and Drama* (London: Hutchinson, 1984).
5 Ibid.
6 McGregor, Tate and Robinson, p. 157.
7 Ibid, p. 23.
8 J. Neelands, *Making Sense of Drama* (London: Heinemann, 1984), pp. 27–32.
9 Dorothy Heathcote in 'Drama as a learning medium', quoted by Alan Howe in *Oracy Matters 5*, Wiltshire Oracy Project, April 1985.

7 Micros and language work

1 I am grateful to Nick Roberts for his assistance in updating this section.
2 Seymour Papert, *Mindstorms: Children, Computers and Powerful Ideas* (Brighton: Harvester Press, 1980).
3 Frank Smith, *The Promise and Threat of Microcomputers in Language Education* (Centre For the Teaching of Reading/Abel Press, 1984), p. 9.

8 Knowledge about language

1 DES, *English for Ages 5 to 11* (The Cox Report) (London: HMSO, 1988).

9 Liaison for continuity, or Les Liaisons Dangereuses

1 Creasey, Findlay and Walsh, *Language across the Transition* (London: Longman/ Schools Council, 1983).
2 Jan Mark, *Thunder and Lightnings* (London: Puffin, 1978), p. 35.

10 The role of the head

1 Quoted in Mike Brearley, *The Art Of Captaincy* (London: Hodder & Stoughton, 1985), p. 278.
2 Case studies 2 and 3 are by heads of 8–12 middle schools.

11 Managing change: the language co-ordinator's support pack

1 I am very grateful to Johnnie Johnson for his contribution to this section.
2 I would like to thank Julie Warne for this case study.

12 Making sense of it all

1 From *The Times Educational Supplement.*
2 I am grateful to David Allen for this material.

Index

READING REAL BOOKS

Robin Campbell

'Real books' have been the focus of controversy as critics argue that the use of real books (rather than reading schemes) in primary schools has caused a downturn in reading standards. The evidence for this is, at best, questionable and the controversy has revealed widespread ignorance of what a real books approach means in practice.

Robin Campbell argues that, in fact, a real books approach is a very demanding one which requires subtle and sophisticated teaching strategies and prior careful planning of the classroom environment to facilitate the management of learning. It is based squarely on beliefs in the power of stories and in children as active constructors of learning as well as in the key role of the teacher. It also assumes that real books are but a significant starting point for a whole range of literacy activities in the classroom.

This is an important introduction to, and argument for, the use of real books as part of a whole language approach to teaching literacy.

Contents
Introduction – Real books – Shared reading – Home–school links – School and classroom organization – Environmental and classroom print – Story reading – Classroom interactions with books – Reading–writing connections – Language experience approaches – Assessment – The importance of the teacher – Postscript – References – Index.

96pp   0 335 15793 9 (Paperback)   0 335 15794 7 (Hardback)

ORGANIZING FOR LEARNING IN THE PRIMARY CLASSROOM
A BALANCED APPROACH TO CLASSROOM MANAGEMENT

Janet R. Moyles

The primary classroom is the context in which a wide range of teaching and learning experiences occur – and not just for the children! What is it that underlies classroom organization, routines, rules, structures and daily occurrences? What are the prime objectives and what influences the decisions of teachers and children? What is it useful for teachers to consider when contemplating the issues of classroom management and organization? What do different practices have to offer?

Organizing for Learning in the Primary Classroom explores the whole range of influences and values which underpin *why* teachers do *what* they do in the classroom context and what these mean to children and others. Janet Moyles draws on several different research findings to examine the evidence in relation to the underlying issues of teachers' beliefs and values. She examines teaching and learning styles, children's independence and autonomy, coping with children's differences, the physical classroom context and resources, time management and ways of involving others in the day-to-day organization. Practical suggestions are given for considering both the functional and aesthetic aspects of the classroom context. Opportunities are provided for teachers to reflect on their own organization and also consider innovative and flexible ways forward to deal with new and ever increasing demands on their time and sanity!

Contents
Introduction: polarizations and balance – Teachers and teaching: beliefs and values – The learning environment: organizing the classroom context – The children and their learning needs: balancing individual and whole class approaches – Grouping children for teaching and learning: providing equal opportunities and promoting appropriate behaviour – Time for teaching and learning – Deploying adult help effectively in the classroom: delegation and responsibility – Evaluating classroom organization and management – Conclusion: the primary classroom, a place and a time – References – Index.

208pp   0 335 15659 2 (Paperback)   0 335 15660 6 (Hardback)

PARENTS AND TEACHERS TOGETHER
PARTNERSHIP IN PRIMARY AND NURSERY EDUCATION

Mary Stacey

This is a practical handbook about how to involve parents in schools, which faces both the problems and the opportunities. Mary Stacey traces the background to parental involvement since the 1960s, discusses the current 'balance of power', and explores how to make schools as organizations work for rather than against parent–teacher partnership. She argues that a whole school approach is important but that it will not work unless the interaction between individual teachers and parents is successful. She examines how to improve communication between parents and teachers, particularly teachers' listening skills; and how to manage in-school meetings with parents, to visit parents at home, and to facilitate the running of parents' groups. This is an invaluable guide for all practising and trainee teachers in primary and nursery schools.

Contents
Part I: Why involve parents? – Beginnings – Teachers: accountable to whom? – Parents: partners or consumers – Part II: What happens in practice? – Into school – Fitting into the organization – Whose school is it, anyway? – In loco parentis *– Part III: Talking together – Communicating with parents – Meetings with parents – Visiting parents at home – Adult groups in school – Adults together – Bibliography – Index.*

144pp   0 335 09435 X (Paperback)   0 335 09436 8 (Hardback)